COACHING GIRLS' SOCCER SUCCESSFULLY

Debra LaPrath

Human Kinetics

Library of Congress Cataloging-in-Publication Data

LaPrath, Debra.
  Coaching girls' soccer successfully / Debra LaPrath.
     p. cm.
  Includes index.
  ISBN-13: 978-0-7360-7212-0 (soft cover)
  ISBN-10: 0-7360-7212-8 (soft cover)
  1. Soccer for women--Coaching. 2. Soccer for children--Coaching I. Title.
  GV943.8.L37 2009
  796.334092--dc22

                              2008024797

ISBN-10: 0-7360-7212-8
ISBN-13: 978-0-7360-7212-0

The Web addresses cited in this text were current as of July 2008, unless otherwise noted.

Acquisitions Editor: Tom Heine; **Developmental Editor:** Laura Floch; **Assistant Editors:** Elizabeth Watson, Kyle G. Fritz, and Laura Koritz; **Copyeditor:** Patsy Fortney; **Proofreader:** Anne Meyer Byler; **Indexer:** Robert Swanson; **Permission Manager:** Martha Gullo; **Graphic Designer:** Nancy Rasmus; **Graphic Artist:** Tara Welsch; **Cover Designer:** Keith Blomberg; **Photographer (cover):** Courtesy of Patti Johnson; **Photographer (interior):** Neil Bernstein unless otherwise noted; photos on pages 7, 13, 18, 30, 39, 48, 56, 168, ©Debra LaPrath; photos on pages 5, 10, 14, 23, 28, 161, courtesy of Patti Johnson; **Photo Asset Manager:** Laura Fitch; **Visual Production Assistant:** Joyce Brumfield; **Photo Office Assistant:** Jason Allen; **Art Manager:** Kelly Hendren; **Associate Art Manager:** Alan L. Wilborn; **Illustrator:** Tammy Page; **Printer:** Versa Press

We thank Maria Carrillo High School in Santa Rosa, California, for assistance in providing the location for the photo shoot for this book.

Human Kinetics books are available at special discounts for bulk purchase. Special editions or book excerpts can also be created to specification. For details, contact the Special Sales Manager at Human Kinetics.

Printed in the United States of America   10 9 8 7 6 5 4 3 2 1

Human Kinetics
Web site: www.HumanKinetics.com

United States: Human Kinetics
P.O. Box 5076
Champaign, IL 61825-5076
800-747-4457
e-mail: humank@hkusa.com

Canada: Human Kinetics
475 Devonshire Road Unit 100
Windsor, ON N8Y 2L5
800-465-7301 (in Canada only)
e-mail: info@hkcanada.com

Europe: Human Kinetics
107 Bradford Road
Stanningley
Leeds LS28 6AT, United Kingdom
+44 (0) 113 255 5665
e-mail: hk@hkeurope.com

Australia: Human Kinetics
57A Price Avenue
Lower Mitcham, South Australia 5062
08 8372 0999
e-mail: info@hkaustralia.com

New Zealand: Human Kinetics
Division of Sports Distributors NZ Ltd.
P.O. Box 300 226 Albany
North Shore City
Auckland
0064 9 448 1207
e-mail: info@humankinetics.co.nz

This book is dedicated to my family for their unconditional love and support, and particularly to my champ, Jared, for his beautiful sense of humor and his willingness to share it with everyone he knows. You constantly remind me of the importance of laughter.

This book is also dedicated to all the soccer players at Maria Carrillo High School—past, present, and future—who have motivated and inspired me on a daily basis to live a life that matters. You have all taught me so much, and I can only hope to have affected your lives half as much as you have affected mine. I know now to appreciate every moment!

CONTENTS

Part IV   Coaching Tactics and Systems

Part V   Coaching Games

Part VI   Coaching Evaluation

FOREWORD

The first FIFA World Cup, held in China in 1991, produced several soccer players who would become leaders and household names: Michelle Akers, Mia Hamm, Brandi Chastain, and Kristine Lilly. Today we have additional role models in Birgit Prinz, Faye White, Abby Wambach, and Hope Solo.

Young athletes now have something to play for beyond collegiate soccer. To keep things progressing, we not only need to continue to foster the participation but also need to develop the fundamentals of the players.

Debra LaPrath and I played and grew up together through the changing times. We were members of the first San Diego County Select Team (now known as ODP), which then became the Surf, the first and only traveling club team in San Diego. We attended and participated in college when recruiting was minimal and there were fewer than 100 NCAA-sponsored women's soccer programs.

Debra is the inspirational player every team wanted. Her enthusiasm, work ethic, and spirit were always a source of motivation at trainings. People simply wanted to be on her team. She brings nothing less to *Coaching Girls' Soccer Successfully*. Her approach to teaching and knowledge of the fundamentals make individuals and teams improve. But what LaPrath really excels at are the off-the-field aspects of team unity, player development, leadership, and communication that consistently build a successful program.

It's no wonder why Debra and I have chosen to spend our lives still involved with the game. Soccer has given us so much over the years— our friendship and our trust and respect for one another. It taught us about toughness, commitment, and, most important, life.

Coach LaPrath continues to have a tremendously successful high school program. Her foundation lies in individual and team development through hard work and respect. *Coaching Girls' Soccer Successfully* demonstrates that this approach breeds success, and any coach can learn from it.

Kim T. Sutton
Women's head soccer coach
Chico State University

ACKNOWLEDGMENTS

I have always been a team player, and like everything else that I've accomplished in my life, this book is the result of team effort. That team effort begins with my family. Thanks to my mom, Joann, and my dad, Alan, for allowing and encouraging me to choose my own path in life and supporting me along the way. Thanks to my sister, Gigi, and brother, Scott. Growing up, I wanted to be just like you, always surrounded by friends and excelling in the sports you loved, especially soccer. Thank you for paving the way with your high standards and accomplishments. Striving for excellence was my only choice. Thanks to my nephews, Jared, Davey, and Jacob, and my niece, Kristiana (Beast). Your sense of humor, passion for life, and love of sports constantly inspire me. Jared, from the day you were born, we had a special connection. You have such a big heart and you make everything fun! Davey, I love your pride. Jacob, nothing gets under your skin (except the word *classic*). And Beast, will you please come play for me one day? You amaze me!

Thanks to all the coaches I have played for and against. You've helped me develop the passion and desire to continue to improve and be a better coach. Thanks to the Sonoma State University team of 1983 and the friendships that still exist. What an inspiring group of people under the passionate leadership of coach Peter Reynaud. You are the team that taught me the true value of loyalty, unity, and hard work. Thanks to Kim Sutton, Patty Carrillo, Theresa Sullivan, and Kelli Robinson for your friendship of 25 years and for still living by those same values. Kelli, your help with the goalkeeping section of this book was invaluable. Thanks to Mary Ellen for always keeping us together. Those dinner parties are priceless!

Thanks to all my players, past and present. The more I gave, the more you gave in return. Thank you for inspiring me daily and making coaching such a fun experience. I can't imagine spending my days doing anything else. We've laughed at the most ridiculous things. The stories are endless and should be a book in and of itself. I am so grateful to the girls at Maria Carrillo High School and the team of 2007 for their support and patience during the photo shoot. You always find a way to make every situation humorous.

All the parents who have entrusted me with coaching your daughters, thank you for the years of support and encouragement. You give your time, you support us financially, and you always fill the bleachers!

Thanks to Katrina Nelson for your continuous support throughout this project. You helped me see the light at the end of the tunnel and encouraged me along the way. Thank you for helping me find the balance and reminding me to put my trust in a higher power.

Thanks to the staff at Human Kinetics, who made this project possible. Special thanks go to my editor, Laura Floch. You made this book the best it could be. Your easygoing demeanor, positive feedback, enthusiasm, hard work, inspiration, extreme patience, and ability to keep me focused truly amaze me! You are a great teacher and coach, and I couldn't have finished without you. We've never even met, yet I feel like I have a great new friend in my life. Thanks to Human Kinetics photographer Neil Bernstein for putting up with us and making the photo shoot a memorable one.

Although this book is written for coaches who love the game, my hope is that you also enjoy it for the stories about the players and the lessons they teach us about hope, passion, struggle, forgiveness, commitment, belief, and the game that feeds us the way nothing else can. After all, that's what it's all about–the intangible things that soccer brings to our lives.

KEY TO DIAGRAMS

GK	Goalkeeper
CB	Center back
LB	Left back
RB	Right back
CM	Central midfielder
LM	Left midfielder
RM	Right midfielder
CF	Central forward
LF	Left forward
RF	Right forward
S	Server
N	Neutral player
P	Any player
O	Offensive player
X	Defensive player

———▶   Path of player (solid line)

- - - ▶   Path of ball (dashed line)

〰〰▶   Path of player dribbling the ball
                       (solid wavy line)

Part I

COACHING FOUNDATION

CHAPTER 1 DEVELOPING YOUR COACHING PHILOSOPHY

As coaches, we are blessed with a rewarding and gratifying profession. We understand the influence we have on our athletes as well as the impact we have on their families and the schools, leagues, or clubs we coach for. Those of us lucky enough to remain in the profession for years understand the impact our athletes have had on our lives as well, and many times we get back more than we gave. It is a consuming, and at times exhausting, job, but exhilarating at the same time. I love the feeling of "the day of the game," and I look forward to what will transpire, who will stand out as a leader, and who will show up with the passion to play "the beautiful game."

This chapter will help you determine the values and principles you want your team to embrace. If your athletes understand their roles and actively engage in individual and team objectives, if they believe and trust in the direction and flow of the team, if they've built solid relationships and have learned how to treat each other and the coaches with respect, then they are on their way to becoming strong, independent, and caring young women.

DEFINING YOUR PHILOSOPHY

Your coaching philosophy should come from your love of the game and the concept of team. It stems from your personal experiences and beliefs and the values you believe are essential, in addition to the type of players you have on your team. Also, as your coaching career continues and you gain experience, and as the players on your team come and go, your philosophy can and should adjust as you stay open to those changes.

When defining your philosophy, ask yourself the following questions:

- What are my values and beliefs?
- What are the individual and team goals?
- What is best for the athletes?
- Am I being true to my own personality?

Above all, when defining your philosophy, keep in mind the concept of developing character. You should help your athletes to continually develop skills that build character. These skills should first emanate from the coaches and captains, but they do not end there. Use drills at practices that test all the girls' leadership styles; this will ultimately lead to a culture your team will embrace. Instilling leadership in all your athletes helps maintain traditions within the program—such as eating lunch together, wearing matching attire, or creating opponent-specific cheers and chants on game days. Athletes become better teammates while sustaining the desire to win. Of course, we all want teams of technically talented athletes, but some of the most technically talented teams do not win championships. Sometimes less technically skilled teams win titles as a result of the close-knit fabric of the team's character.

The Significance of Team

Several times a season, we run a character development drill in which the girls line themselves up based on their influence on the team, allowing them to define *influence*. We then spend time debriefing the activity. We ask the players why they chose their positions. The girls give many reasons, such as talent, ability, leadership, mental and emotional attitude, aggressiveness, commitment, playing time or the lack of, dedication, and work ethic.

After this dialogue, we give the girls 60 seconds to take a position based on where they would want to see their mom, dad, or sibling on the line of influence. If there are changes (and there usually are), we ask them why. Do they expect more, less, or the same of a loved one than they do of themselves? Over the years I have seen teams do this activity many different ways. I've had teams line up without talking, teams that couldn't agree on positions so players overlapped and wouldn't budge, and teams that joined hands in a circle, refusing to identify one person as more influential than another. We always learn a lot about the character of the team while the girls learn about each other.

Finally, as mentioned previously, it is important to remain flexible when defining your coaching philosophy. Like life itself, your season will go through unforeseen changes. Athletes may change schools or decide to play different sports, injuries might occur, motivation and desire can fade, stormy weather can impede your games, or the quality of officials can change the outcome of a game. Being flexible does not mean you are giving up your convictions and beliefs; it simply means you do not stress over the things you cannot control.

DEVELOPING YOUR COACHING STYLE

All of the coaches I had growing up influenced me in various ways. I admired the coaches who let their personalities show while maintaining discipline and structure within the team. These coaches had a strong desire to win, but they truly had fun with the game. They were also the ones who had us over for dinner!

One of my college coaches taught us that sacrifice and a bit of suffering would take us to greater heights both individually and as a team. He would train us so hard we could barely move, but then he would invite us over for dinner at the end of the practice. After one particularly tough practice, one of my teammates literally could not move from the table after dinner; her legs just didn't work. We laughed hysterically.

This type of training makes your players rely on each other, take care of and look out for each other. A strong sense of camaraderie develops when your players are giving everything they can for the sake of the team. They see each other at their worst and at their best. A style like the one that my college coach exemplified created a closeness that fostered respect between players and coaches and encouraged us to be ourselves and let our personalities guide us. We were learning some of life's greatest lessons, but more important, we all felt that we were a part of something bigger than ourselves. The result of those experiences is that, 20 years later, those teammates are still my best friends!

When athletes are encouraged to be true to who they are, they discover the strengths and traits that make them unique. By developing their unique qualities together with their teammates, they set standards for the team and focus on the principles of character that they know are important, such as trust, respect, dependability, and humility.

Now that I'm a coach, I strive to imitate the qualities and characteristics that I admired in the coaches I had growing up. I've certainly adopted styles from past coaches, some more than others. I think most coaches can't help but take bits and pieces from the influential coaches in their lives and turn those into their own personal styles.

ESTABLISHING OBJECTIVES

Once you've defined your philosophy and developed your coaching style, you need to be clear about your objectives for yourself, for each member of the team, and for the team as a whole.

Objectives for Yourself

As a coach, you should stay true to your strongest character traits and strive to improve on those qualities that don't come as naturally to you. If you focus on your strengths and lead with good character, you'll be confident in your abilities and continue to seek excellence both on and off the field. Following are some elements to consider as part of your overall objective:

- *Staying current in the sport of soccer.* Consider joining professional organizations affiliated with soccer and coaching, such as the National Soccer Coaches Association of America (NSCAA) or the American Sport Education Program (ASEP). You can also subscribe to magazines that focus on coaching and teaching in general. There is a wealth of information online for every soccer component, such as drills, systems of play, and player development. In addition, spend time reading books by successful soccer coaches and players such as Anson Dorrance and Mia Hamm. Books written by coaches of other sports, such as Pat Summitt and John Wooden on basketball, can also have a powerful impact on your coaching style and philosophy. Sometimes, though, your best resource is your own experience. Trust your intuition, which comes from your own playing and coaching experiences and knowledge of the game.

- *Trusting yourself and the decisions you make for your team.* It takes practice to make decisions in stressful, split-second situations. Just as your athletes must practice making decisions based on game situations, you'll need to practice listening to your inner voice. Get into the habit of writing down when you've made good decisions based on your "gut feelings," to help you learn how to trust your instincts. In chapter 2, I

When communicating with your team, focus on recognizing areas for improvement, acknowledging what the team does well, and praising individual stand-out performances.

explain a program in which I require each girl on the team to keep a folder of reflections on performance and competition. Just like my athletes, I keep a folder to record game-day thoughts, team moods, energy levels, and the degree of focus at practices and other team events. These entries help me keep track of what is happening with individual players as well as the highs and lows of the team. I also find it helpful to talk with my coaching staff and other mentors in my life to gain perspective.

• *Providing a secure environment for your athletes.* Your athletes need an environment in which they are allowed to fail. Rather than criticize them, critique them to help them improve (for more information, see Communicating with Players on page 9 of chapter 2). Teach your athletes to think for themselves and become confident decision makers. They, too, need to learn how to trust their intuition, and they can only do so if they have the freedom to take chances and make mistakes.

Individual Athlete Objectives

Because the girls on your team may vary in age and maturity level, their personal goals should also vary. On a high school team, for example, seniors will have different goals than freshmen. College, scholarships, work, and moving out on their own can weigh heavily on their minds. Respect their personal goals as long as they don't interfere with the team's goals. If you have a player who is focusing on just her personal or school life, you might have her fill out a separate goal sheet for soccer, stating what she would like to accomplish for the season.

Athletes should have both short-term and long-term goals. Short-term goals are what they hope to accomplish in the first half of the season; long-term goals are what they hope to accomplish by the end of the season and beyond.

Following are tips for helping athletes set goals:

• Have them list their goals and objectives and a paragraph or two of how they visualize meeting their goals.

• Have them list ways they can determine whether they met each goal.

• Have them prioritize their goals and create positive affirmations for their most important goals.

• Have them give a copy of their goals to you, and plan to monitor these goals often during the season and record their progress in meeting these goals.

• Have each athlete give a copy of her goals to a teammate. Halfway through the season, the teammate can evaluate whether she has achieved her goals.

In addition, you should have nonnegotiable expectations of your players based on the standards and values that are important to your coaching staff and the traditions of the program. These are behaviors that you want your players to focus on both in their personal lives and on the soccer field. Following are some examples:

• Be responsible and respectful.

• Be on time and be dependable.

• Be honest with your coaches and your teammates.

• Represent your team, school or club, and community with pride.

• Always work hard and maintain a winning attitude.

• Be respectful to officials, opponents, and teammates.

• Develop a leadership role based on your own strengths.

• Always put the team before yourself.

Team Objectives

Coaches who do not include the athletes' perspective when developing team objectives inevitably find themselves alone in the pursuit of those goals. Do not try to micromanage this process. Whether you are developing objectives for the season or a particular game, the athletes need to know that their voices count!

The Importance of Spirit

Sometimes players start the season with a particular position or role in mind and then redefine it as the season progresses. One such player was Leah, our backup goalkeeper, who was more than content with her role. She was always eager to get the starting keeper warmed up at practice or before a game, and she was a verbal leader for the rest of the team and enjoyed getting people fired up for games. When the opportunity allowed us to put Leah in and get some playing time, she said she didn't really want to go in. I had never had a player tell me she didn't want to get in the game, but it was evident from her tone that Leah was telling the truth. She said she'd rather focus on the team from the sideline and not focus on her own game.

Leah had become more of an assistant coach than a player. She loved the camaraderie and friendships that soccer brought to her life, and that was enough for her. She cared little about the game except for how others were playing and whether we were winning. Leah was a motivating and positive force on the team, and she embraced her role with enthusiasm.

When Leah "tried out" for the team again her senior year, I had to decide whether to take her, a player who didn't want to play, or give her spot to another athlete. Making her a manager was not going to cut it; she would not have felt she were truly a part of the team. The decision really was not difficult to make; of course, I took Leah! The athletes and I were all better because of Leah's love of life, not soccer.

As you and your team work to develop team objectives, explain that they are defining some-thing that is greater than the vision or desires of one person and that taking on an attitude of selflessness and service to each other will help create a strong, well-connected team with individual and team accountability. As a coach, your role is to guide them in focusing on what they want, not on what they don't want. The feelings behind the objectives are just as important as the words used to define them. They must truly believe in their objectives to see them manifest. Following are some examples of things to consider when developing your team objectives:

• *Maintaining respect.* Young people, especially girls, can have a lot of rules when it comes to defining their friends and whom they associate with. Often they dislike people they don't even know based on reputation or hearsay. Remind your girls that although being friends with each other is important, the most important factor is treating each other with respect both on and off the field through their actions and their words.

• *Being honest.* Teach your athletes how to be honest with each other. Tension off the field can turn into tension on the field and potentially affect game situations as well as team dynamics. Talk to the girls about convictions and explain that you do not tolerate double standards. If they want their teammates to be honest with them, they must be honest with their teammates.

The day before a big game, keep things lighthearted at practice to help calm players' nerves.

• *Learning to forgive.* Every season inevitably has problems and setbacks. Players become academically ineligible, get injured in practices and games, and struggle with friendships. The greatest mistake you can make is to ignore these problems. You must be willing to deal with uncomfortable emotions and confront negative situations. When problems are confronted and out in the open, the players learn to deal with difficult issues, reach compromises, forgive each other, and move forward with their focus on the team's goals. One of the signs of a successful season is athletes who have truly learned empathy for each other.

• *Learning the importance of self-discipline.* Self-discipline helps athletes believe in themselves and gives them the confidence to take risks. Self-disciplined athletes influence the entire team by believing they deserve success because of all the hard work they have put in. This attitude will carry your team through setbacks and difficult times. Ultimately, being a coach is about shaping your athletes' lives so they are capable of making good decisions on their own. By embracing these values, your athletes will learn to achieve more than they ever thought possible.

• *Enjoying the process.* We've all been in situations in which we are so focused on the result, we forget to enjoy the process of getting there (for more information on how to keep the sport fun, see page 18 in chapter 3). When athletes are focused on results only, they become stressed and anxious. They are afraid to make mistakes and therefore play tense while focusing on things they cannot control. Allow your athletes the freedom to fail and take risks. Redirect their focus to the things they can control such as their courage, enthusiasm, and work ethic. They will become more confident players by focusing on performing at their best for themselves and their teammates.

• *Building strong relationships.* When teammates build strong relationships, they experience the cohesion and sense of unity that can help them achieve their goals. To maintain these relationships, athletes must learn to define and accept their roles on the team. You can help by encouraging them to become passionate leaders, while setting realistic personal goals. This way they continue to have a purpose for working hard.

• *Prioritizing what is important.* Even the most dedicated athletes appreciate the coach who doesn't make soccer the most important thing in their lives. The preteen and teenage years are confusing and emotional, and girls need guidance making decisions on how to manage their time and commitments. I encourage my athletes to prioritize in the following order: health, family, school, soccer and other sports, and friends. This doesn't mean I expect less from them when they are with me, quite the opposite. I expect them to be in the moment and to give fully of themselves because they have taken care of the other things in their lives. Although girls learn valuable lessons and develop lifelong relationships through soccer, soccer at this level is not life!

CHAPTER 2 COMMUNICATING YOUR APPROACH

Communication is the key to success in any organization. Because we communicate in many ways—through body language, facial expression, and vocal tone—it's important to pay attention to what the situation dictates when communicating with athletes. In addition, communication is not one-sided; rather, part of the art of communicating is being a good listener. It's also important to read people correctly, especially when they aren't saying anything at all. When players are clear about your expectations and their roles on the team, they will have greater success within the program.

COMMUNICATING OFF THE FIELD

Learning how to communicate effectively with those involved in your program is vital for building supportive relationships. In addition to your players, you will need to interact with parents, administrators, and the media.

Communicating With Players

How you communicate with your players off the field has a major impact on how they'll respond to you on the field. Away from the field,

your role is more that of a listener or at times a caretaker. Sometimes just knowing she's been heard is enough to settle an uneasy player. You can't always resolve your girls' concerns, but you can make time to listen. Following are a few ways you can communicate with your athletes off the field:

• *Meet with the athletes individually.* Take the time to meet individually with each of your athletes before the season begins and continue throughout the season every few weeks or when time permits. During this time, you can learn about their personalities, what they want and expect out of the season, and what motivates them in difficult situations. Also, spend time talking about individual objectives or goals and how they can meet them. Ask them for their input about practice sessions and what they need to help them improve. These one-on-one meetings do not need to be formal; they can be between classes, on the way to a game, or after practice.

• *Write to your athletes.* Writing to your athletes throughout the season is another effective way to communicate with them about their lives away from the soccer field. It also gives you another venue to express how you feel about their contributions and obligations to the team. You can write letters or e-mails or use their folders, as discussed later. Because everyone is unique in how they communicate, the better

Take time to develop team unity and cohesiveness by bringing your players together before each game and allowing them to visualize and affirm their strengths and commitments to one another.

you know your athletes, the easier it becomes to communicate with them appropriately. If you really take the time to learn about your players, you can integrate the game plan for the season with what's important in their lives.

• *Criticize constructively.* Criticizing your athletes constructively is an art. You must find a way to correct athletes' mistakes, attitudes, and behaviors without destroying their confidence. To do this, you'll need to know what motivates them. Also, remember that no two athletes are alike. Some want you to get after them in certain situations; others take criticism personally. Talking in a harsh tone to those who are more sensitive and already lack confidence may cause them to become even more discouraged. Following are three ways you can change negative criticism into something positive:

1. Whenever possible, let your athletes play through mistakes without pulling them from the game. If you pull them directly after a mistake, they will play tentatively and begin to lack confidence in their ability.

2. Make sure you are criticizing the behavior or action and not the person. Behaviors

and actions can be corrected; anything else will be taken personally.

3. Use the sandwich approach when giving constructive criticism: Start your feedback with a positive comment, then give instruction on what they need to correct, and finish with a positive statement. For example, "M.J., I really appreciate how hard you're working, but when you're the last defender, try to contain the attacking player and wait for support. Don't reach in and try to steal the ball. You're a great defender, and we need you out there!" This gives the player proper feedback for correcting her mistake, but at the same time recognizes her effort and her contribution to the team.

• *Use your captains.* Captains can help you communicate with your athletes when important announcements need to get to the team immediately, such as practice or game changes, transportation issues, and other general information. They can make announcements over the school bulletin, divide the team into groups and use their cell phones to text announcements for lunchtime meetings, or gather the players for group meetings in the team room. Your captains can do in five minutes what would take you triple the amount of time.

Folders for the Team

At the beginning of each season I put together a folder for each player. The folders consist of a cover page, game schedules, tournament schedules, contact information, schedules for team social events, statistics sheets, commitment contracts, affirmation and goal worksheets, rankings, newspaper articles about the team, quotes, and lined paper for weekly assignments. Every week we gather with the folders to discuss goals, talk about our objectives for the next game, read quotes and discuss their meaning, and review the week's writing assignment.

The quotes I pass out at our weekly gatherings are based on themes I see my team struggling with, such as discipline, belief, friendship, leadership, or opportunity. We also spend time discussing a topic of the week, such as rivalries, mental imagery, characteristics in players and positions, game preparation, or positive thinking.

I also give my players weekly writing assignments. Sometimes they exchange folders with other players and write about what they appreciate about each other and what their teammates bring to the team both on and off the field. I may ask them to write to me about their role on the team. I might give them questions to answer, such as: Who do you consider a clutch player on this team? What makes you the most secure? What is your biggest worry? What is the most honest thing you have done? What inspires you? or What does playing with intensity look like?

The personality of the team guides me in deciding what to discuss and ask them to write about from week to week. Over the years I have seen players open up to their teammates in ways they never had before or discover new ways of expressing themselves. Their relationships with each other are strengthened, and loyalties are formed. Their words of encouragement to each other foster confidence and a closeness that is hard to define.

Past players have expressed to me the importance these folders have had in their lives. Parents have even told me that their daughters have taken their folders to college to stay connected to their past, to inspire and motivate them as well as remind them to stay true to themselves.

Communicating With Parents

Many parents, especially those with sport backgrounds, want to be involved in their daughters' activities. When communication between the coaching staff and parents is successful, parents have a better understanding of their role and how they can best assist the program.

Prior to the season, after tryouts are completed and the team is selected, hold a parent meeting to discuss your coaching philosophy and individual and team expectations. The purpose of this meeting is to introduce yourself and the coaching staff and to make parents aware of the requirements and obligations that both they and their daughters have to the team. Make it very clear that you want parents around and need their support in guiding the team to a productive and fun season. This is also the time to ask for their help and support in a variety of ways, such as the following:

- Compiling a list of team names, phone numbers, street addresses, e-mail addresses, and other related information
- Organizing a schedule for working the gate and snack bar at games
- Helping with fund-raising activities at games and other school or community events
- Driving to games and practices at special locations
- Hosting weekly dinners at their homes
- Preparing the field and equipment for games
- Attending athletic committee meetings

Involving parents will help you develop a positive rapport with your athletes, and it will help you keep the lines of communication open. Parents should feel comfortable approaching you to talk about their daughters, and being involved with the team can make them feel more comfortable. Parents who are around the sport as volunteers interact more with the coaches, learn more about the game, and get to observe their daughters' personalities as they interact with their coaches and peers. Being involved also gives parents the opportunity to learn more about you on a personal level, showing them that you care deeply about their daughters and have their best interests at heart.

Parents sometimes naturally have their own agendas for their daughters. As a coach, you have to make decisions based on what's best for the group. Because you may not always be able to tell parents what they want to hear, it is vital to have a good working relationship based on communication and mutual respect.

Make a point early in your season to stress to parents that they should not be communicating for their daughters at this age. Players need to talk to you directly about their concerns, abilities, and playing time rather than using parents as middlemen. This doesn't mean that you cannot discuss things with a parent; you can, but only if it is for their peace of mind and not the athlete's.

Communicating With Administrators

Clear communication with your administrators is necessary to prevent any miscommunications about eligible athletes, academic expectations, practice and game-day procedures, student injury and liability, and the overall success of your program.

You may need to communicate with your administrators about things ranging from a student's grades to a change in a game time that will affect busing. Administrators are there to support you both on and off the field, and they appreciate it when you run an organized program and communicate clear expectations to your athletes about how they must represent your school or club. Following is a list of ways to communicate effectively with administrators:

• Learn how to communicate your situation before it becomes a crisis, giving administrators ample time to handle the situation. It helps to stay organized and use a journal or file to keep track of any situations that may require administrative support.

• Respect that administrators often wear several hats and are very busy people. Most athletic directors, for example, are teachers first. They have commitments to their classrooms in addition to the athletic programs. If you work with your athletic director, respect

his or her commitments, and communicate your needs in a timely manner rather than expect immediate action, you will find him or her more willing to work with you to meet the needs of your team.

• Know that you may not always see eye to eye with administrators. At times you may need to compromise to find common ground, such as when several teams need to prepare for games on the stadium field at the same time. Be willing to work with the other coaches and athletic directors so everyone is getting a fair shot at field use.

• Be reasonable in your requests. The administration will appreciate your not asking for more than you need. For example, if you are going to exceed the amount budgeted on uniforms because of the type of uniforms you want, make up the difference with your team account, and let the administration know what you are doing.

• Be mindful about following the chain of command. When asking for something, follow the proper procedures. Do not go over someone's head to accomplish a task. Fill out the appropriate paperwork, if necessary, and ask the right people to do the job. This includes all people in all positions. If you have a request or a question about the restrooms on the field, talk to the head custodian first; don't immediately complain to the principal. Complaining about a situation before dealing with the people responsible alienates them and undermines support for your team.

• Keep your administration informed about activities and team plans outside of school. Invite them to games, team dinners, fund-raisers, and end-of-season banquets.

Communicating With the Media

You should be teaching your athletes how to communicate with adults in a respectful and appropriate manner. If you genuinely emphasize this, then your players will be prepared to have a healthy rapport with your local media. When communicating with the media yourself, keep the following in mind:

In addition to the media, call on your parent volunteers to help photograph and videotape your games.

- Focus your comments on your own team's performance rather than that of the opponents. That way you will not have to worry about saying something that can be misconstrued.

- Provide the media with rosters so that they have the proper spelling of your players' names. Also provide them with your contact information and the best time to reach you.

- Let the media know the results of a game as soon as possible, particularly if you are the home team.

- Take time to establish a good working relationship with the media. Their coverage can help your athletes with the exposure needed for scholarships.

- Teach your athletes how to keep comments about opponents positive, complimenting their opponents' efforts. Remind your athletes to keep their comments short so that they don't get trapped into lengthy dialogues about opponents.

- Emphasize to your players and fellow coaches the importance of humility. Everyone on the team should be able to talk about her

performance in a humble manner without sounding arrogant.

COMMUNICATING ON THE FIELD

There are two main groups of people you must communicate with on the field: your players and the officials.

Communicating With Players

Off the field, your role with your players may be more of a listener or caretaker. On the field—in practice and game situations—your role becomes that of a teacher of many things, from the technical and tactical to the physical and mental.

Practice is a good time to introduce your athletes to high-pressure situations they may encounter in games. If they've seen the situation in practice, they won't panic in games because they know what to expect. For example, practice penalty kicks in ways that simulate game situations, such as having the player walk to the penalty kick spot, kicking the ball on the whistle only, knowing without question the proper placement of the top five kickers, and having the other players be silent during the kick. This way, players will be clear about their roles and have the confidence to take on the task before them.

In games, you should not be thinking for your athletes by yelling out their every movement and pass. They need (and typically only hear) short commands that give simple instructions and the motivational words to get them through the demands of competition.

When communicating to players during the game, project confidence with your voice and body language. They do not need to see you looking worried in a tense situation. Stay positive and speak with conviction. Your athletes will feed off your emotions, both your calm confidence and your enthusiasm. Learn to read your team in various situations so you can provide the balance between getting them fired up and calming them when their emotions are running too high.

The Rap Connection

Coaching books often focus on the communication between coaches and athletes. I have found that it is equally important to teach my players how to communicate effectively with each other. I encourage honesty and trust within the team, and I expect players to confront each other when there is a problem and then work together to find a way to move forward. I have also found that giving the players a little time to catch up on each other's lives outside of soccer helps maintain an open dialogue within the team structure. I also give them time during the warm-up at the beginning of practice or during the pregame stretching to chat with each other on a personal and social level.

When communicating with each other, players sometimes have their own language. That's all right with me, although I don't always understand it or agree with it! During one game, two of my most skilled players—with leadership skills to match—didn't seem as focused during the warm-up as they typically were. I started them anyway, but soon had to pull them out of the game. I was disappointed in their performance and made sure they knew it!

Later, as I focused on the game, I heard sounds from the bench that I didn't recognize. As I listened more closely, I realized it sounded like singing. I couldn't believe it. Did I really have players sitting on the bench singing during an important game? Could they really be that disrespectful? I glared toward the end of the bench only to find the two players rapping with each other—sharing verses, moving their hands, and going all out! I stormed over to them and, in my sternest voice, said, "What do you two think you are doing?" Their response was: "Coach, you don't understand. We're trying to feel each other; we weren't feeling it out there."

I wanted to explode. I sent them to the other end of the field and told them if this was how they were going to get inspired to play together, I didn't want to hear it. Every once in a while I'd glance at them over there rapping and it really began to make me laugh, although of course I was not going to let them know that.

I didn't understand their way of communicating with each other, but I did trust them. Through hard work, we had developed a rapport, and a little rap was not going to change that. In short, you cannot always control how players are going to connect with each other. Sometimes you need to let go and let them find their own ways to communicate.

Communicating With Officials

During your season, you will ultimately encounter every type of official—those who let the game get out of control and are constantly out of position to make a call, and those that control everything and won't answer a single question. The best games occur when you have officials who can find the balance between controlling the game and communicating with the players and coaches. With these officials, regardless of the outcome, at least everyone can agree that it was called fairly. This doesn't mean that you will always agree with the calls that the officials make or that you won't argue an occasional call. However, you must do so in a manner that shows that you respect what they do. Teach your players that it is your job, as the coach, to discuss calls with the officials. When you cannot

It's in everyone's best interest to remain professional when discussing calls with officials. Respect them and understand that they are trying to be fair and honest.

converse with them, then it should become the captains' responsibility.

Even though only you or your captains should discuss calls with the officials, teach all players on your team the difference between confronting an official and simply asking a question. Explain that tone and body language play a huge role in communicating with officials. Also, remind your athletes that constant complaining will get them nowhere and that they should never put their energy into worrying about the officials. They need to learn how to stay focused on the game and not allow a few bad calls to take away their focus and concentration. I expect the players to be respectful and not let their emotions dictate their rapport with the officials. We are all passionate about the game, including the referees; otherwise, they wouldn't be out there.

Sometimes keeping your composure is difficult when you have invested so much in a game and you believe an official is manipulating it. I'm not going to discourage being passionate during a game, but excessive emotion can work against you. Like your athletes, you need to learn to stay calm in challenging situations.

CHAPTER 3 MOTIVATING YOUR PLAYERS

Motivating athletes is one of the greatest challenges we face as coaches. Regardless of whether you are coaching at the youth, high school, or collegiate level, the story is always the same: You will have experienced teams that are extremely talented but lack true motivation and teams that are slightly less talented but highly motivated. You have before you a group of young ladies of various age, maturity, and skill levels, and all are at different stages in their athletic careers. In addition, each responds differently to various styles of motivation.

So where do you begin with each new season? You begin with you! You must set the example for what you want from your athletes. Do you show up on time? Are you prepared to run an organized practice, or do you wing it? Is your energy level high? Are you genuine when greeting your athletes? They will know whether you've taken the time to prepare and whether you're excited to be their coach.

It is your job to show up focused, excited, and ready. Your players deserve that, and they will most definitely feed off your energy. Be consistent in your mood regardless of how well the team is playing, its win–loss record, or what is happening in your personal life. If you expect your athletes to be consistent, you need to display the same type of behavior. Your attitude toward the team determines to a large extent what you get back from your players.

You can't lead others to places you don't want to go yourself.

CREATING A HEALTHY TEAM CULTURE

The best motivation techniques in the world are not worth their salt if you have not established a healthy team culture of mutual trust, respect, and fun. The best way to do this is to get to know your players on and off the field, make soccer fun, and let your players make decisions that affect the team whenever possible.

Knowing Your Players

When your athletes sense that you understand and care about them, they will feel that the team is their team rather than your team. As a result, you will have an easier time keeping them inspired. If you coach from the heart, they will play with heart.

Many activities that you do outside of practice or games can give you and your team opportunities to get to know each other in an open and supportive environment. By having the team eat lunch together on game day, for example, you give them the opportunity to check in with each other prior to meeting in the team room. As a team they can also make sure they are taking care of themselves by properly fueling up before the game.

The more you know about your athletes, the easier it will be to motivate them to play. By earning your players' respect and trust, you will foster an environment in which they aspire to perform to the best of their abilities and take responsibility for "their team." As a result, they will hold each other accountable for actions and behaviors that affect the team.

Making Soccer Fun

One of the primary reasons athletes quit playing sports is that they aren't having any fun. Many that don't quit lack the motivation to work hard. Athletes are motivated when they are having fun and enjoying success. Success comes from feeling satisfied about their performance and believing they are making a worthy contribution to the team. The truth is that you are not directly responsible for motivating your athletes; rather, you are responsible for creating an environment in which your athletes motivate themselves and each other. You can do this by making training fun and challenging and using rewards when appropriate to help build intrinsic motivation in your athletes. Following are some ways you can help keep soccer fun for your athletes:

- *Teach your athletes how to deal with stress and anxiety.* Visualizations, affirmations, and positive self-talk can be powerful tools for athletes who are feeling overwhelmed (for more information on these concepts, see chapter 6 on page 43).

- *End practice sessions with drills or games that your athletes enjoy, or allow your athletes to design a practice.* I let my high school seniors pick a practice to organize and run.

- *Change your practice environment.* Train indoors or at another facility. I sometimes give my team a tough conditioning session at the beach. This provides a fun atmosphere while they put in maximum effort.

- *Create competition within your drills and activities.* Group players in a variety of ways, such as grouping seniors against the rest of the team, playing defensive players against offensive players, or even grouping players by birthday months or favorite foods. Establish point values and give the winning group an external award, such as gift certificates for smoothies or free team T-shirts.

- *Encourage and allow time for laughter.* Enjoy your girls' individual personalities. Spend time together by organizing team dinners or volunteering to set up for events hosted by the school. You and your athletes put in too many hours during a season playing a sport that you love not to get a true sense of what it means to have fun.

- *Go with the flow when possible.* As coaches, we sometimes show up with our to-do lists and try to force our agendas based on what we think the team needs. Pay attention and stay in tune with your girls' moods and needs. Sometimes you may need to change or put away your agenda based on the group's energy level. This does not necessarily mean that you

Training at the beach, if you are fortunate enough to have one nearby, is a great way to bring variety and fun into your practice sessions. Your athletes will enjoy connecting with one another and working hard in the cool, salty air!

accomplish less; you just go about your lessons in a different way.

- *Create an atmosphere of support and encouragement.* Allow your players to see your personality and how much you enjoy working with them. Show up each day with enthusiasm while checking in with your players and asking about their days.

Involving Players in Team Decisions

Allowing your athletes to be part of the decision-making process makes them feel more accountable for their successes and failures. Being involved in simple decisions such as the design of your pregame T-shirts or who will be team captains helps them to feel more committed to the team.

There are so many ways to involve your athletes. You may allow veteran players to provide feedback on which new players make the team. Although you don't give them the authority to cut players, you could listen to their opinions. Having opportunities to be involved in decisions like this helps all of the athletes on the team become more responsible for each other, which translates into holding each other accountable for individual performance. When a veteran player has pushed for a particular new player and that player is not playing up to her potential, the veteran player may feel responsible for checking in with the new player and offering support and feedback.

TYPES OF MOTIVATION

Motivating your team never ends; it just changes form from season to season, not to mention month to month or even day to day. Many of your athletes show up to practices and games motivated for various reasons—they love the game, they enjoy the friendships, they're in a good mood, or they crave competition. However, a long season can dim even your most enthusiastic players. This is where your creativity comes into play.

Motivation is useless unless you have first worked on mutual respect, as discussed earlier and in chapter 1. Team pride develops on its own in an environment of mutual respect, and what better motivator is there than a prideful team? If your athletes know you respect them, they will accept your criticism and suggestions with an open mind. They may not like it, but they will respect your opinion and not hold a grudge. We've all heard the adage, "Treat people the way you want to be treated." Lack of respect between players and coaches, or among players, breeds conflict and can be a surefire way to kill team unity.

This section addresses three ways to motivate players: using goals, effective practices, and reinforcement.

Using Goals as Motivation

Setting goals for both individual and team performance is a great way to motivate athletes, as long as the goals are realistic. Far too often, coaches set individual performance goals that only the best players on the team can realize. Your athletes must learn how to set realistic goals for themselves first and then contribute to the team's goals. Unrealistically high goals usually result in failure! Individual goals should focus on specific performance or behavior, rather than winning or losing. When athletes set realistic personal goals, they have more control over their successes and take more responsibility for their failures.

Many athletes learn to judge their athletic success based on winning or losing. Help them understand that true success lies in achieving their own personal goals rather than measuring up against other players. When athletes focus on their personal goals and contribute to the team the best they can, team goals take on a different meaning. The team goal can then become respecting each other, learning to play together as a group, having fun, always giving their best, and practicing good sporting behavior. When your athletes feel confident in meeting their individual and team goals, they will be motivated to work hard. When that happens, winning takes care of itself.

Team Goals

Teamwork is not something that comes naturally to a group of people. It involves sacrifice and putting aside personal agendas for the good of the team. You have to teach teamwork to your athletes. Just because they love the game of soccer doesn't mean they are going to work with or for each other. They come in thinking they know how to be good teammates, but every season a new group joins the team and the dynamics are changed, which means goals need changing too. If you've done your job well, returning players will make the new athletes feel welcome and equal in their influence on the team. If that type of chemistry is in place, then setting tangible team goals is that much easier.

Every team wants to win a championship, but if your primary goal is winning, then you tend to ignore the short-term goals that get you to the championship game in the first place. Establish a vision, a long-term goal that you never lose sight of, but focus on smaller goals one training session and one game at a time. One way to do this is to adopt the 24-hour rule. Spend no more than 24 hours agonizing over a loss or celebrating a win; then look at what you can correct and move on.

Following are examples of short-term team goals:

- To force corner kicks in every game when we are strong in the air

- To communicate with each other and keep communication positive

- For everyone to know and understand their jobs during set plays

- To work hard in practice and bring out the best in one another

- To actively work toward improvement on a daily basis

- To share in the responsibility of encouraging one another daily in practices and in games

As the season progresses, so do the dynamics of your team. What may have motivated them in August will change by October, so naturally you will need to revisit your goals. In the beginning of the season, your team goals should be based on fitness as well as developing relationships. Once games begin, set goals for each game, making sure you don't look too far ahead but rather prepare for the next game only. It's very easy to overlook a generally weaker opponent and then pay the price.

In the training sessions that precede a game, break down what you know about your opponents and look at your own strengths and weaknesses. From there you can set specific performance goals based on your objectives for that particular game. For example, if your forwards focus only on scoring goals and don't succeed, they see their game as a failure. When athletes disappoint themselves too often, a lack of self-confidence sets in. A more realistic goal for your forwards would be to commit to working hard to win the ball back when they lose it on the attack. This high pressure on the ball from the attacking players helps support the team in a number of ways, and it becomes a tangible, team-oriented goal.

Smoothies for Success

During practices, I often hold competitions in which my players compete for ranking on the team by performing technical skills such as dribbling, shooting, passing, and heading. Top-ranking players are rewarded with certificates for smoothies. Sometimes I bring smoothie menus to practice and pit the defense against the offense. The winning teams get to choose the flavor of the smoothies and pretzels that I will deliver at the next light training session. These small incentives often fuel the last 20 minutes of practice when the athletes are beginning to get tired and settle for lackluster performances.

Individual Goals

As mentioned in chapter 1, taking the time to set individual goals is an important part of working together as a team. However, individual goals do not necessarily motivate every player. Because you cannot force individual goal setting on all your athletes at this level, sometimes the best you can do is encourage individual goal setting and leave the rest to the athlete. On the other hand, some players really understand the value of goal setting and thrive on achieving and re-evaluating their goals.

Again, as mentioned in chapter 1, one-on-one meetings with your athletes can help facilitate the goal-setting process and open up a dialogue that will help them narrow their focus. Some players are afraid to set goals for fear of disappointing themselves and, in turn, their teammates. In their minds it is "just easier to play and not stress about all that." Such players need help understanding that being accountable to themselves and their teammates is a crucial part of being on the team. Help them see that they need to be responsible for their failures as much as their successes and that setting goals is one step toward achieving that.

Breaking their goals into smaller pieces helps athletes take responsibility for their goals without getting bored along the way. Consider the use of folders, as discussed in chapters 1 and 2. Rather than having your players state or write out personal goals for an upcoming game, have them write visualizations of a particular play going a certain way. Instead of writing, "I'm going to score in tomorrow's game," which is an outcome a player may not achieve, she can simply visualize, or describe, scoring in a specific play. Encourage the girls to write freely in their visualizations, including specifics such as smells, sounds, weather, the feel of the field, and the names of some of their teammates.

I've been fortunate enough to witness players' visualizations become reality on the field. When that happens, they look at me wide-eyed and full of disbelief. It is an amazing accomplishment for the athlete. Because their minds have already worked out the details of a play, they are more likely to see it through physically. These are the teaching moments I wouldn't trade for anything.

Reading as a Team Sport

In the spring prior to our fall season, I meet with the athletes who are going to try out for soccer. At these meetings we go over the usual information regarding summer camps, tryout dates, fund-raisers, and fitness goals. These meetings are also the time to discuss their summer reading! Players must choose one of two books to read, and prior to tryouts they will need to pass a written exam on the book they have chosen. The books are not necessarily about soccer; rather, the underlying concepts can translate into any sport or endeavor, such as survival, leadership, determination, responsibility, attitude, and team concepts.

Aside from the obvious benefits of having my athletes continue to read in the summer, the book assignments help in many ways. Throughout the season the team can use many of the concepts they learned from their readings. Believe me, there is a lot to be said for 22 athletes sharing teaching moments because they've read the same book. In addition, the summer reading assignments give us a head start to the season and allow us to connect instantly after having spent several months apart. Following are several books that I have assigned over the years:

- John Maxwell's *The 17 Essential Qualities of a Team Player*
- Lance Armstrong's *Every Second Counts*
- Pat Riley's *The Winner Within*
- Michelle Akers' *The Game and the Glory*
- David Beckham's *Both Feet on the Ground: An Autobiography*
- Jere Longman's *The Girls of Summer*
- Pat Summitt's *Raise the Roof*
- Kyle Maynard's *No Excuses*

Using Practice as Motivation

Used correctly, your training sessions can be your best motivator. Training hard gives players that edge in knowing that, when all else fails, they will have "muscle memory." Although they may not be able to control the final outcome of the game, they can be assured that they will not be outworked by their opponents. As the saying goes, "Hard work beats talent, when talent doesn't work hard." Here are a few examples of strategies for motivating athletes in practice:

- *Creating competition.* Competitive games or drills combined with incentives can motivate your players if you create an environment in which they know they can compete against one another without worrying about feelings getting hurt. At this level, your athletes may not understand that it takes practice to develop a competitive mentality and that competing against their teammates is a safe way to do just that. Remind them that if they don't compete with each other in practice, they won't be prepared to do it in the game.

- *Ensuring variety.* Working on technical and tactical aspects of the game can consume the majority of your practices. Taking the time to ensure variety in your practices will keep your players interested. Combine technical drills with fitness and team-building activities. When planning technical sessions, rather than focusing on only one concept, use drills that combine skills. When appropriate, use drills and games that you know your players love, introduce new ones that you think they'll enjoy, and allow them to select their favorite drills or games to end a practice session.

• *Encouraging team building.* Team-building games and activities keep athletes motivated in practice. One of the most important things I've done over the years is add mental and moral conditioning to my players' physical conditioning. Athletes need to be conditioned in all areas, including mentally and emotionally.

• *Keeping things exciting.* Keep practices moving with little down time when transitioning between drills. When athletes are not challenged, they become bored; if the challenge is too great, they become anxious. Keep practices flowing with appropriate challenges that test their limits, and maintain realistic expectations of their performance when teaching something new.

First at the Pasta Feed!

Each season, the players and coaches of our team need to get to know and trust one another. The motivation to work hard and perform at our absolute best is easier when we are working with people we truly care about. Our team holds weekly pasta dinners, called pasta feeds, which contribute to our relationships with each other and help create an overall team chemistry. Parents sign up at the beginning of the season for weekly dinners on the evening before the big game of the week. After practice we load into cars and arrive at homes where parents have prepared incredible meals for the players and coaches. Once everyone has arrived, players serve themselves class order: seniors first, then juniors, and so on. This tradition continues from year to year without me having to enforce it. It's another privilege the seniors look forward to. Now, being first to eat may not seem like a big deal, but when you've been at school all day, practiced for two hours, and are facing trays of lasagna, spaghetti, salad, and garlic bread along with 22 hungry athletes, being first is an honor and a welcome treat!

Using Reinforcement as Motivation

Your athletes will need both verbal and nonverbal reinforcement to build confidence and motivate them to continue working hard on behalf of the team. This reinforcement can be critical when an athlete is going through a difficult time and just needs to know that someone is there. Reinforcement is also important when you see your team going through a tired or uninspired phase. During such times, let your players know how much you appreciate their efforts.

Verbal Reinforcement

Verbally communicate your expectations to your athletes and encourage them to ask questions if they don't understand those expectations. I've had a lot of players who learned early in their playing careers that asking questions resulted in either their teammates thinking less of them or their coaches screaming at them. As a result, they learned to not ask questions for fear of humiliation. Make sure your players know that they have the right and the responsibility to ask questions when they don't understand.

Verbal communication with your players can come in many forms; it can be general comments directed toward the team as a whole or individual praise either one on one or in front of the group. There is no right or wrong way; it depends on the situation. Obviously, athletes respond differently to verbal praise and constructive criticism. Knowing what buttons will send your athletes over the edge is important. However, it's more important to be consistent and fair and not let their emotions dictate your response. You'll always have athletes who are more vulnerable and sensitive than others, but you're not doing them a favor by treating them more softly than the rest of the team. You must find the balance between your verbal praise and constructive feedback.

Following are some ways to use verbal reinforcement to motivate your athletes:

• Call out players' names with common phrases such as "Great job" or "Way to dig deep." When athletes hear you say their names, they are reminded that you are paying attention and appreciate their efforts.

• Give the players nicknames and use those names as much as possible; this helps personalize your relationship even more. Then, when your athletes hear you use their regular names, they know you mean business!

• Provide specific feedback on an athlete's individual skills so she knows why you are complimenting her; you can also combine your compliments with something she needs to work on. For example, you could say, "Great shot, and remember to follow through on your kicking foot."

• Hold one-on-one conferences. These sessions can be informal and brief. Meet with players for a few minutes after practice just to check in and see how they're feeling, or call them on the phone in the evening for a short dialogue. I like to have one-on-one conversations with players on the way to pasta feeds or before and after games.

• If you are a high school coach, organize and oversee evening sessions with veteran players to help them write college letters. This can be an opportunity to help them make choices about their college education. As I mentioned earlier, writing to players in their folders is another great way to give them individual attention.

• Call an athlete at home after practice or after a particularly good performance in a game and compliment her on what she did well. This will show that you recognize her importance to the team. This can also help build self-confidence and lets her know that her efforts will not go unrecognized.

Also note that it is just as important to encourage verbal communication among teammates. This can have a huge impact on team spirit. Encourage your players to "catch" their teammates doing something good and to let them know right then and there, whether it's in a practice or a game. Athletes often believe they have an edge over a team whose members are verbally critical and condescending to one another. Point out that praising and verbally supporting each other can have the opposite effect: making their opponents believe that they are emotionally connected and working together.

Nonverbal Reinforcement

There are ways other than the spoken word to communicate to your athletes and motivate

Reinforcing and acknowledging your athletes' work ethic and dedication is a great way to motivate them to continue their commitment to the team.

them to perform at their best. Body language is an easy way to convey exactly how you are feeling about a given situation. Sometimes all it takes is a look or a heavy sigh to let your players know what you are thinking. A high-five or a pat on the back is a simple gesture that gives athletes that much needed approval without needing to say a word. Introduce your players to the saying, "What you do speaks so loudly, no one can hear what you say." This will communicate your respect for the importance of nonverbal communication and having a positive attitude.

Adding time to drills or transitioning quickly into conditioning in response to a lackadaisical performance can inspire a little more intensity or concentration in your players. Changes like this can be made with little or no verbal communication, and it doesn't take long for the lightbulb to go on.

In soccer, we do not have the luxury of timeouts to discuss strategy; we generally have to wait until halftime to communicate with the team as a whole. On occasion I don't hold the typical halftime talk; instead, I make my captains responsible for the dialogue. This is my way of telling the girls that I have nothing to say because the team has yet to follow through on what we discussed prior to the game. When the players see their captains coming to meet them at halftime without me, the message is loud and clear. Saying nothing at all lets them know exactly how I'm feeling about their performance.

The Team of 2000

I generally avoid talking about previous teams' accomplishments and critiquing past seasons with the current team. Although much can be learned from previous mistakes, I do not like to spend too much time in the past. Occasionally, however, I tell the story of the team of 2000. It was a team of very talented players who truly worked well together. This was a team that had to win! They were hard on themselves without me ever having to say a word.

Overall, this team was a fun group of girls who believed in themselves and had good chemistry combined with high expectations. As we approached the postseason with an undefeated record and a scoring frenzy of 102 goals and only 12 goals against, we were starting to get a lot of attention. ESPN called and asked to come out and do a segment recapping our season.

Representatives from ESPN came to our training session and interviewed some of our top players. They also attended our pasta feed that evening and filmed the players having dinner and socializing. The following week we all watched the segment with excitement. As if that weren't enough to continue to drive this team, a sports magazine did a cover story on our goalkeeper and defense that came out in October, just prior to the play-offs. At that time, we held the number one spot in the NSCAA national high school rankings for the third straight week. Life was good.

But like all successful teams, we had rules, and when rules are broken, consequences must follow. One Friday evening after a game, four players decided to drink alcohol at a football game, and I found out about it. I immediately called each player and told her she had to go to the principal Monday morning and tell him what happened, and to be prepared to no longer play for the team. I followed up with a phone call to the athletic director, and she in turn let the principal know what was going to happen come Monday morning. I let the players know that if they failed to go to the office before school, I would personally bring them when I arrived for practice.

I spent the rest of the weekend sick to my stomach. This was no longer about soccer games; this was about personal responsibility, honesty, and owning up to the consequences of your actions. That Monday we lost four starters and a huge part of the heart of our team. Yet, I was blessed with the responsibility of now making the 16 remaining players understand what was before them and convincing them that they had worked too hard to let the actions of a few destroy what they had worked for. We went on to win our last league game and advance to the final round of sectionals before losing in the final game 2-1. We finished the season 21-1 and lost our top national ranking with that final game.

As painful as that final game was (I still have not watched it on tape), we all learned so much from that season. I'm a better coach because of it. Three of the players returned the following season and came in with a new mentality. They were going to make sure everyone knew about that painful mistake and the lesson they learned about self-discipline. They came back prepared to take on true leadership roles. What would I change about the team of 2000 if I could? Nothing. I did everything I could have done given the situation. There's no pillow so soft as a clear conscience. I sleep well at night.

CHAPTER 4

BUILDING AND MAINTAINING YOUR SOCCER PROGRAM

A successful soccer program is measured by its long-term impact on the athletes, school or club, and community. Many coaches excel in the technical or tactical aspects of coaching, or both, but a few winning seasons does not necessarily equate to a successful program. Successful programs require attention to management responsibilities such as establishing rules and disciplinary guidelines, securing assistant staff, gaining support from the administration, and creating traditions and team pride. These responsibilities can seem overwhelming, but ignoring them can cause your team to deteriorate before the season has even begun. If you take the time to create and implement an organized and functional system for your program, your management responsibilities will not take away from the main reason you're in this profession— to coach the game and make a positive impact on your athletes' lives.

DEVELOPING A SYSTEM

To build a successful system for your soccer program, you will need to establish rules based on your coaching style, your philosophy, and your objectives, as discussed in previous chapters. You will also need to make decisions about your team personnel and learn how to use these positions to achieve what you want from your program.

Establishing Rules

Your school, district, or club may have guidelines that the athletes must follow to be a part of your soccer team. These guidelines ensure that all participants have a fair, safe, and rewarding experience in their sport. At our school, for example, the girls and their parents are given an "athletic clearance packet" with forms they must complete and policies they must read before the girls can try out. Included in the packet are academic requirements, an athlete's code of conduct, a medical insurance information form, health history and health exam forms, an athletic eligibility screening form, transportation forms, ejection policies, as well as a team pledge. Once they have turned in the packet, the girls receive a clearance form stating that they are eligible to play. Note that most sports affiliated with a school or club provide handbooks that state their policies and procedures and provide the necessary forms that the girls and their parents must fill out in order to be eligible to participate in athletics. Typically, schools provide these forms because of liability and legal issues. If for some reason a handbook is not provided, contact your school or district for forms.

School, district, or club rules and guidelines can be very thorough in regard to academic requirements, attendance policies, sporting behavior, and citizenship. However, you should also expect your athletes to follow other rules, such as the following:

- Be on time to practices, meetings, and games.
- Check in with one another and say hello.
- Help set up and clean up equipment.
- Call the coaches in advance if you will be missing a practice.
- Bring your folders to all weekly dinners.
- Use "Please" and "Thank you" whenever possible.

Avoid creating rules at random or unnecessarily. Remember that the fewer rules you have, the fewer rules your girls will break. Too many rules requires that you implement a lot of consequences, which can put both the coaching staff and the athletes on edge and set the girls up for failure. Keeping the rules to a minimum will make them easier for the players to follow and allow the coaches to be coaches rather than rule administrators.

Establishing Discipline

Inevitably, rules will be broken, so make sure you've established disciplinary procedures and appropriate consequences for breaking rules ahead of time when you are clear-headed rather than having to create them in the heat of the moment (for example, see figure 4.1 for a school team pledge that each player and parent or guardian of the player sign prior to the start of the season). The consequences that you set should be the same for every athlete on the team so that everyone is treated fairly and consistently. In addition, you must be firm in your consequences and follow through with them; otherwise, your word will mean very little to your players. If you tell a player that she must turn in a progress report on Monday or she will not play in the game on Wednesday, then that's

---

Team Pledge

I, _____, as a member of _____, recognize the importance of adhering to team rules. As a member of a team, I realize that I must make a commitment to myself, my teammates, my coaches, and my school, and that this commitment entails strong self-discipline. I recognize the clear fact that I cannot perform up to the high standards that are expected of me if I indulge in the use of alcohol, marijuana, performance enhancing drugs, or any other controlled substances during the season. I further realize that to do so will jeopardize my eligibility because of state, federal, and school board regulations. My signature on this statement is a symbol of my strong determination to be the best athlete that I can be at _____. My signature is my word that I will adhere completely to a commitment to zero alcohol/drug use during this season. Furthermore, if I fail to comply, I will immediately report the incident to my coach and accept the disciplinary action from the coach and his/her staff.

Player signature: _____ Date: _____

Parent/guardian signature: _____ Date: _____

Courtesy of Maria Carrillo High School

From *Coaching Girls' Soccer Successfully* by Debra LaPrath, 2009, Champaign, IL: Human Kinetics.

Figure 4.1

what needs to happen regardless of who the athlete is or what team you are playing. Allowing the athlete to play because you think you need her conveys to the athlete that there is bargaining room when it comes to consequences. Now imagine how hard it will be to get a progress report next time!

Through the course of your coaching career, you will encounter disciplinary situations in which you feel the athlete deserves a second chance. Other situations will be cut and dry: The athlete takes the consequences and the team moves forward. Sometimes the only recourse you will have will be to remove the athlete from the team.

You may encounter novel situations for which you don't have specific rules. For example, one season we had a player who had gone through a rough time the semester prior and was ineligible, so she could not try out for the team. Once school started again, she worked really hard and brought her grades up quickly, so we had the option of bringing her back on the team halfway through the season. But would that be fair to all the athletes who had worked hard to make the team and earn playing time? I had never dealt with this situation before, so there were no specific guidelines in place for this decision. I decided this decision was not mine, but rather the team's. We called a team meeting, and the captains ran it. My fellow coaches and I initially opened the meeting by telling the team we would support their decision either way, and then we left. We did not want the players to hold back their feelings about the situation and worry about what the coaches would think. The team decided to let the player join the team, giving her a second chance and rewarding her for turning things around.

Allowing your athletes to be involved in creating the disciplinary process can help hold them accountable. When athletes help in setting the disciplinary standards for the team, they want to cooperate because they put those standards in place. Captains and veteran players can be responsible for holding the younger players accountable. Younger players respond to these expectations because they admire and respect the veteran players and do not want to disappoint them. When included in the disciplinary process, players gain confidence knowing they are in control and are capable of dealing with

their problems. You end up with a team with the self-discipline and conviction to stay the course when times get tough.

Teaching your athletes about discipline—especially self-discipline—should also be a primary objective, as discussed in chapter 1. Far too often, young coaches confuse discipline with punishment. Punishment is a consequence for breaking a rule; discipline is self-control. You provide a much healthier environment if you talk with your athletes about exhibiting self-control rather than threatening them with punishment. Teach your athletes about the discipline it takes both physically and mentally to be at the top of their games so they can develop character while learning self-control. Discipline will help your athletes get through a game when they are tired or stay focused on their goals while learning to cooperate with their teammates. With discipline also comes accountability. Disciplined teammates will hold one another accountable for doing what's best for the team.

One of the greatest challenges you will face as a coach is teaching your athletes how to make disciplined lifestyle choices. Many young athletes deprive themselves of sleep or proper nutrition, or spend a lot of energy on boyfriend and friendship problems. Then there's the ever-present issues of alcohol and drugs. If your focus is on developing self-discipline, then you are fostering leadership qualities in your athletes and they will begin to discipline one another. Once they are convinced that developing self-discipline and leadership is in their best interest, you'll need to teach them that it will take time. Our society teaches us the opposite—that things should happen immediately. When we don't see results overnight, we lose patience and give up.

Establishing Team Personnel

Once you have established your system and have your school's support in the guidelines for your program, it's time to address personnel decisions. You will need to determine who your assistant coaches will be and whether to have student assistants or managers, and you will need to choose your captains. Once these positions are filled, work closely with your team personnel to set the tone for the upcoming season.

Pregame meetings with officials and your opponents should be a positive experience and one that sets the tone for the game.

Assistant Coaches

Finding and keeping assistant coaches is not easy, especially if the position is unpaid. Regardless of whether your assistants are paid or are volunteers, make sure they have the best interest of your athletes at heart. Two important characteristics to look for in assistants are loyalty and trustworthiness. You should be able to trust that they support your values in guiding the team. That does not mean requiring that your assistants act and think like you, however. They should have their own thoughts about how the game can and should be played. A coaching staff with similar values and vision, but different perspectives about the game, is healthy for everyone involved. You don't want all your players to be the same; you also don't want your coaching staff to be clones of one another.

Diversity of gender can also be helpful. I try to have a male assistant because I believe that a male perspective can be an important attribute on a team of young women.

Assistant coaches with strong convictions who are willing to speak their minds are an asset to the team. Disagreements among the coaching staff are fine, as long as they do not happen in front of the players. A successful program is about cohesion. If you stick to the values and principles that you have established, then long-term success is inevitable.

Captains

Your captains can help you develop the spirit and dynamics of your team. They should share the vision that you are working to create for the team and should take on the responsibility of generating enthusiasm within the team.

Captains' responsibilities can include starting practice and pregame warm-ups and organizing equipment setup and cleanup. They should also help you set the tone and intensity level in practice and in games. Captains also help organize team activities and are the team's spokespeople when dealing with officials during games.

If your captains trust and respect your judgment, they will feel comfortable telling you when problems arise on the team. Explain to them the importance of keeping you informed when problems are getting blown out of proportion, but encourage them to try to handle team conflicts on their own when appropriate. Also, explain the importance of talking to troubled teammates without judgment.

You should feel comfortable relying on the leadership of your captains. Make sure you communicate with each other constantly and focus on encouraging and complementing them as much as possible. Because the responsibility can get overwhelming at times, talk with them about the importance of giving and receiving, while taking the time to take care of themselves.

As a coach, you must allow your captains to find their own voice rather than hover over every decision they make. They will learn through trial and error how to put emotions aside and make decisions based on the team vision. When they need your guidance, provide it; otherwise, give them the opportunity to develop into leaders and realize who they are and what they stand for!

Big Willie

Big Willie was a captain for our team who epitomized selflessness and devotion to the team and had an enormous work ethic. Although she also ran track and was extremely dedicated to her academic career, she continued to participate in the soccer program. She was always warmed up and ready to sub in if the opportunity arose, yet she never complained if it didn't happen. Not one to sit on the bench, she usually stood beside me enthusiastically giving her valuable support and input. She trusted my judgment and always wanted what was best for the team, even if it meant a lack of playing time for herself.

Big Willie easily made the varsity team as a freshman, but sadly, her playing time became more limited later on after she suffered a concussion. However, she gained the respect of her teammates and coaching staff by maintaining program traditions, keeping a positive attitude, and remaining focused on the team goals and the game. Her teammates continued to vote her captain throughout the years, even though her playing time significantly decreased. Big Willie's leadership, work ethic, and selflessness made a lasting impression on the future leaders of our team and set an amazing example of what a captain should be.

Starters and Reserves

The relationship between starters and reserves can either foster or hamper the way your team works together and communicates. If you think the dynamics of those relationships don't affect the team, think again! I've seen it tear great teams apart. Teamwork is something that must be developed; it does not come naturally for most teams. At this level, starting matters, and it is your job to clarify the criteria for starting. It is also your job to clarify the role of the reserves.

Many variables can affect a starting lineup. Players get injured or become sick, become ineligible because of poor grades, or are put on probation as a result of misbehavior. Typically, because most players work hard enough to start, you must consider talent and team chemistry when creating your starting lineup. For reserves, the greatest challenge you will find will be continuing to develop their self-confidence.

Continued lack of playing time usually results in lack of confidence. In these situations it is important to teach your athletes about belief—belief in their ability to focus and work hard and belief that they belong out there and are capable of being successful on this team.

Having athletes define realistic roles for themselves is another way to bridge the gap between starters and reserves. Remind players that defining their roles on the team does not mean that those roles won't change. By defining their roles, players can examine where they are within the structure of the team and where they want to go.

Explain to your players that starting positions can be won or lost during practice sessions, and thus, every practice is a new opportunity. Players should know that their pregame warm-up can dictate whether they start. Players who normally start cannot afford a lackadaisical warm-up. If they do get complacent, often spending time on the sideline at the beginning of a game is enough of a wake-up call! Tell them that you expect the intensity in their warm-up to emulate their enthusiasm for the game. I'm not talking about foolish, obnoxious intensity, but rather, a focused, competitive energy with a will-to-win mentality. Talk about the difference between those emotions and how to maintain focus. If you address these warm-up expectations with your athletes beforehand, there will be no confusion when you announce the starting lineup.

Open communication is important with all your athletes, but particularly with your reserves. Emotionally, they need the support of your coaching staff and the team. They need to be encouraged at practice to challenge not only themselves but the starters as well. If they are fighting for a position, then they should be one of the toughest teams the starters see all season. Typically, reserve players will be very emotional when approaching you about playing time. Genuinely listen to them and offer suggestions on ways they can continue to contribute to the team vision. Remind them that their ambitions and those of the team are not separate and that they are all in this together. Do not feel you have to fix the problem for them. Be supportive and encouraging. Help them to stay focused on supporting the team while striving to meet their personal goals.

IMPLEMENTING THE SYSTEM

Spending the time and energy developing a system for your program does not guarantee its implementation. Implementing the system requires gaining support for it and instilling tradition and pride in your athletes.

Gaining Support

Support for your program is an integral part of your team's success. For this reason, you must have a good relationship with your school's or organization's administration, as discussed in chapter 2. Let them know what you stand for and explain the expectations you have for your athletes and the standards you hold them to.

In addition to gaining support from your administration, you should also gain community support. One way to do this is to create a relationship with your local newspaper and stay in touch with journalists throughout the year, during both the season and the off-season. Most local papers will print local schools' game schedules as well as scores and statistics from each game. Many papers also have special sections for Athletes of the Week, or give athletes press when they have made college commitments or pursued other athletic endeavors.

It is also extremely important to partner up with local businesses when possible. This can sometimes be difficult because many businesses are constantly bombarded with fund-raising requests. However, when asked, most will try to support you in any way they can. You can give them credit for their support in a number of ways. For example, you can have banners made and hung in your stadium, put their company name on T-shirts or water bottles, or print an advertising poster with their business cards along with your team photo and game schedule. By selling the product, you can advertise for them all season long. Businesses can use their donations as tax write-offs if you follow up with

Support from family and your community during games encourages athletes to be positive role models and to perform at their best.

a thank-you letter that includes your school's or organization's tax I.D. number. It's a win–win situation!

Former players can have a great impact on your current team. Alumni who come to work with or speak to your team can be a terrific source of inspiration for younger players who may have been in the stands at one point watching them play. If those alumni have had successful college careers in soccer, their presence is even more powerful. They continue to pass down the pride and tradition of the program to their younger siblings, cousins, and neighbors.

Alumni can also be some of your greatest supporters at games, fund-raising efforts, and school events. If enough former players are in town, an alumni game in the summer can be a great way to raise money and encourage alumni involvement. The important thing is to stay in touch with as many of them as you can and persuade them to give back to the program. If you've fostered good relationships with your athletes, you will not have to seek them out. Many will stay in touch with you as the years go by. You may eventually find yourself being used as a reference for jobs and attending college graduations, weddings, baby showers, and family events.

You can also invite young players to come and cheer for your team. One season we had the support of a six-and-under team at home games. One of the girls on the team was the daughter of a former player. With their screaming and cheering, those five- and six-year-old soccer players made our high school team feel like World Cup players. That kind of community support and enthusiasm is infectious!

Creating Tradition and Pride

Traditions passed down through the years help build team unity and create pride in your program. They may be simple, such as teammates eating lunch together on game days and using pregame cheers and songs during warm-ups. Other traditions could include weekly team dinners or keeping personal folders, as mentioned in previous chapters. Whatever the traditions might be, encourage them. However, remember that traditions do not win games in the long run. The foundation of your program and the underlying principles remain the same: hard work, honesty, integrity, a team-first mentality, strong leadership, and true enthusiasm for the game.

If you've taught your players well, then they really play for each other. If honesty, respect, and hard work are values you expect from your athletes, then that is what you will get. With these expectations, you can instill pride in your athletes and your program while avoiding a sense of entitlement. Far too often kids believe they are entitled to receive without earning. Respect is earned through honesty and hard work. It is essential that you have this type of dialogue with your athletes so they learn what you stand for.

Part II

COACHING PLANS

PLANNING FOR YOUR SEASON

In addition to coaching your team, you are responsible for many aspects of your soccer program, including the budget, facilities and equipment, policies and procedures, and schedule. Before your season begins, it's a good idea to take time to do some planning. By organizing early, you can avoid the last-minute scrambles that can divert your attention from coaching when the season begins. You will have peace of mind knowing your program is well thought out, and your calm confidence will influence your fellow coaches and athletes.

ORGANIZING RESPONSIBILITIES

A yearly to-do list will keep you organized and help you group your responsibilities into manageable chunks. It will help you stay focused on your vision and give you time to enjoy working with your athletes rather than focusing on all the tasks you need to accomplish.

A good place to start is to divide your year into off-season, preseason, in-season, and postseason; then break this down even further by listing the months that fall under each category. List the things you need to accomplish during each month. You can even break down your monthly to-do lists into manageable weekly lists. When you have all of your tasks on paper, you will be able to see which responsibilities you can easily delegate to your assistant coaches and eager parents.

The sample yearly plan shown in figure 5.1 is broken down into months and phases of the season—off-season, preseason, in-season, and postseason. Not all teams will follow this format, however. For example, some states allow for organized off-season play, and therefore the time line for those coaches would be different.

Try to prioritize your responsibilities so you don't have to do everything at once. For example, if it's only one month prior to your season and you have not ordered equipment, scheduled your postseason games, or made travel plans for tournaments, you will find yourself overwhelmed and most likely unable to complete these tasks to the best of your abilities. Keep in mind, too, that even if you are organized and following your timetable, plans can change as a result of unforeseeable circumstances. Therefore, it is important to allow yourself some flexibility within your to-do list. Also, take the time to reassess your list from year to year and make the appropriate changes that will benefit your

Sample Yearly To-Do List

Off-season

January	
Attend conferences or clinics	Meet with administration
Read books for summer reading program	Research tournaments for travel
Evaluate program	Work with athletes on writing college letters

February	
Attend conferences or clinics	Call vendors about equipment and uniforms
Continue search for summer reading	If traveling, talk with tournament officials
Begin scheduling preseason games	Continue to write college letters with athletes, plus hold open homework sessions
Look for new fund-raising ideas	

March	
Begin budget work	Order equipment and uniforms
Continue preseason scheduling	Set up meeting with feeder schools
Reserve hotels for travel	Hold homework and tutoring sessions

April	
Confirm hotel reservations if traveling	Finalize preseason schedule
Review conditioning program	Type and print alumni game flyers, and confirm alumni addresses
Meet with players to hand out information on summer reading, summer soccer camps (on and off campus), fund-raiser obligations, athletic packets, and physicals	Hold homework and tutoring sessions

May	
Submit preseason schedule to athletic directors	Set date and send out flyers for alumni game
Meet with parents to discuss travel plans	Hold homework and tutoring sessions

June	
Type and submit final game schedule to athletic directors, referee's association, and local newspaper	Hire summer soccer camp coaches
	Continue work on reservations for travel
Collect fund-raiser cards and money from athletes	

Preseason

July	
Meet with athletes attending summer soccer camp	Check field conditions and equipment
Conduct weeklong off-campus camp	Print alumni and camp T-shirts
Follow up with players and physical forms	Get uniforms and bags numbered, if new
Submit fund-raiser cards to printer	Hold alumni game and hold barbecue

Early-to-mid August	
Conduct on-campus summer soccer camp	Prepare final conditioning program and team bonding experiences
Measure and paint fields; check goals	

In-season	

Mid-to-late August	
Conduct tryouts and hold first official practice of the season	Hold captain and senior meetings
	Schedule all weekly team dinners for the season
Finalize and submit roster to athletic directors	Prepare individual player folders
Attend referee and league meetings	Meet with parents to delegate jobs
Hold individual player meetings	

September	
League games begin	Organize writing assignments and topics of discussion for team dinners
Organize game promotions and recruit ball girls for home games	
	Recruit parents to photograph and videotape games for review and banquet slideshow
Plan travel for tournament if scheduled	
Copy weekly newspaper articles and quotes for team dinners	

October	
Submit all applicable playoff forms	Get baby photographs from senior parents for senior dedication
Check grades	
Reevaluate first half of season	Conduct playoff meeting last Sunday of the month
Prepare for last senior home game	

Postseason	

November	
Playoffs	Prepare team and senior dedication slideshow for end-of-season banquet
Order awards and type certificates for end-of-season banquet	

December	
Hold end-of-season banquet—decorate and organize food	Work with athletes on writing college letters
	Evaluate yearly to-do list and timetable for next season

Figure 5.1

program. Following are a few points to keep in mind as you organize your responsibilities for your season:

- *Don't take on too much too fast.* Begin by doing those tasks that you do well and then take on other tasks based on deadlines or guidelines set by your school or organization or your season.

- *Manage your time.* Often we underestimate how demanding and time-consuming management tasks can be. When you're feeling overwhelmed, slow down, prioritize what needs to be done first, and enlist help from others. Again, look at your to-do list and focus on the immediate task at hand.

- *Make time for yourself.* Time away from the field can help you regroup and concentrate on something other than soccer, or it can give you time away to review what you've accomplished and where you're going. A day or two away from the field can be refreshing for both the coaching staff and the athletes.

- *Use your resources.* Many resources from several organizations, such as the American Sport Education Program (www.ASEP.com), the National Soccer Coaches Association of America (www.nscaa.com), Positive Coaching Alliance (www.positivecoach.org), and Character Counts (www.charctercounts.org), can help you with the seemingly overwhelming task of managing your season. Do not be shy about asking for help from your support staff, particularly your assistant coaches. Your team managers and athletic directors are also there to help, so do not be afraid to delegate responsibilities.

REVIEWING THE BUDGET

When you initially begin coaching, you have to anticipate your financial needs for the season. Rest assured that once you've been doing it a while, it becomes easier! If you've taken the time to properly inventory equipment and uniforms at the end of each season, then your job will be easier as you begin your planning for the next season. You must first decide what items are most important for your program and budget for those items first. Obviously, basic equipment needs, such as uniforms, balls, cones, and high-quality goals and nets, are most important

and should be your priority. It makes sense to purchase high-quality equipment that will last longer. I'd rather have six good balls over a dozen cheaper ones that need to be pumped up every hour because they don't hold air. You will also need to consider the costs of team travel.

To help with your expenses, you can undertake fund-raising activities such as community and alumni donations, summer soccer camps or clinics, silent auctions and dinners, and rummage sales. You can advertise for businesses that contribute to your program by printing T-shirts or banners to hang at home games, publicity posters with business cards, or discount cards. You can also print your own labels for water bottles that have your school logo on one side and the sponsoring business logo on the other side. Another source of funds can come from your school's booster club for athletics.

How to spend your fund-raising dollars is another important decision. Some items to consider are team sweats, bags or backpacks for each player, socks (not usually a budgeted uniform item from the school), practice and pregame warm-up T-shirts, and hooded sweatshirts for those cold nights. Other items include specialty training equipment such as mini-goals, flags, hurdles, ladders for footwork, and medicine balls.

EXAMINING FACILITIES AND EQUIPMENT

Your season can ultimately be limited by facilities that are in poor condition or a lack of equipment. Be proactive and assess the quality and availability of your facilities and equipment prior to your season, so that you can take the steps necessary to get things in top condition for your season.

Your facilities are typically maintained by the maintenance crew at your school or club. Unfortunately, the condition of your facilities largely depends on your school's or club's overall budget. If maintaining the fields during the summer months is not a priority for your school or club, when you return in the fall, the fields can be dry and hard, then get overwatered and become muddy as the maintenance crew tries to make up for lost water time.

The bottom line is that you need to have safe and playable fields. If your fields are in poor condition, you must communicate your concerns to your athletic directors and administration. Ask them to walk the fields with you so that you can point out specific conditions that, if left unattended, could become safety concerns and could potentially end the season early for one or more of your athletes.

You'll also need to ensure that you have plenty of equipment available for the start of the season and that the equipment is in working condition. Again, the time to begin this is the end of the previous season. Get rid of old equipment and take the time to inventory what can stay in storage until next season. This way, when it comes time to order new equipment, you know what you need to buy. Following is a list of equipment, some necessary and some to help run a variety of training sessions for your athletes.

- *Balls:* Regulation game and practice balls (minimum one per player)
- *Ball bags:* Typically two to three bags, depending on size
- *Scorebook:* One per season
- *Wipe-off boards with dry erase marker:* One per season; can be reused from season to season
- *Cones:* Three dozen minimum
- *Flags:* One dozen minimum
- *Vests:* Two or three colors; twelve of each color
- *Nets and clips for goals:* One good-quality net for each goal; at least 20 clips per goal
- *Agility ladders and rings:* Two ladders, twelve rings
- *Medicine balls:* Two or three
- *Resistance bands:* Two or three
- *Mini-goals and mini-hurdles:* One set of mini-goals and two dozen mini-hurdles
- *Multitouch balls:* Six minimum
- *Water coolers and bottles:* Two coolers, twelve bottles minimum
- *Uniforms and sweatsuits:* One for each athlete; two extras for emergencies if possible
- *Individual bags or backpacks for athletes:* One per player

Communicating and working with your administration, custodians, maintenance crew, and parent volunteers are vital to maintaining a great venue for home games.

In addition, you should always have a medical kit available, along with ice and water. Inventory your medical kit at the end of each week so you can replace what you are low on before an emergency occurs. Your administration or athletic director can provide the basic supplies you will need, such as tape, prewrap, bandages, gauze, instant cold packs, peroxide, scissors, sterile pads, and tape adherent (spray). You may need to purchase additional items out of your own funds such as tweezers, eyewash, tampons, ibuprofen, and heat therapy gels—all important items for teenage girls!

Above all, teach your athletes to take care of their equipment and take pride in their facilities. This is an area you will not regret spending time on. If you allow athletes to throw tape or garbage on their own field after practice and games, they will treat other facilities the same way when playing away from home. Disrespect for facilities either at home or away should be unacceptable. This is not a difficult battle to fight if you are firm in your convictions. Once the girls see what you stand for, they'll begin to take on those characteristics themselves.

REVIEWING POLICIES AND PROCEDURES

When organizing for the start of your season, you'll also want to review your team policies and check for any changes in policies from the organization that governs your school or district competitive events.

Eligibility

Academics is a topic you should discuss often with your athletes and emphasize at your first parent meeting. Let parents know that the athletic directors will keep you informed about players' eligibility status and that you may be asking athletes to do weekly progress reports if they are on academic probation. Explain in detail the way the progress reports work; most parents don't know unless they've been through it with another child. Also make sure they have the school schedule for tutoring and homework clubs so they know what type of support is available for their daughters. When parents, teachers, counselors, and coaches communicate with each other, student-athletes are less likely to make excuses for poor grades.

Medical and Emergency Support

Medical support is extremely important in contact sports. Many school districts and organizations either don't have the funds to have an athletic trainer on staff or have not made it a priority, which is surprising in this age of lawsuits. If you don't have an athletic trainer on staff, as a coach, you need to stay current in first aid and take courses in the athletic training field. You can also search your community for students who are studying to be athletic trainers and need to put in some volunteer hours. Student trainers, with district clearance, can assist in taping and treating minor injuries. However, in the event of a more serious injury, always seek professional medical attention.

Athletes and their parents or guardians must sign the proper forms giving them permission to compete as well as provide medical insurance information. If parents do not have medical insurance, the school district will provide information for students who qualify to enroll in no-cost or low-cost health insurance programs. If an athlete sustains an injury that requires professional medical attention, you have a responsibility to fill out a student accident report immediately following the injury. You should also follow up with a phone call that evening to find out how the athlete is doing. Ultimately, the health (both mental and physical) and safety of the athlete should be foremost in your mind.

SETTING THE SCHEDULE

If you have the freedom to decide which teams to play in the preseason, remember to balance your schedule with teams that will challenge your players and teams that will help your players gain confidence. Of course, if you have a veteran team that has the potential to do really well, by all means schedule games that will challenge them to the fullest. Regardless of your team's potential, though, it is a good idea to schedule games against the top teams in your classification, because you will most likely see them in play-offs.

Courtesy of Jared Braden

Traveling out of state provides the opportunity for your athletes to experience various cultures, develop relationships with athletes from other teams, and gain recognition by competing against nationally ranked schools.

If you want to play different teams and give your athletes exposure to college coaches and if you think your team has the potential to make the national rankings, then playing teams from out of state is a good idea. Developing a rapport with specific out-of-state teams can allow you to share the cost of travel on a rotating basis. For example, we have been fortunate to develop a relationship with the folks at Houston High School in Germantown, Tennessee. They have arranged two trips to California in the past seven years, and while it's been a lot of fun hosting their team for games, dinners, and sightseeing activities, it is our turn to travel to them. While making plans to attend their tournament we are already experiencing their southern hospitality. Playing teams from around the nation who have had great success over the years in their state tournaments can benefit your team in so many ways.

Aside from the benefits of competing against top teams from other states, the relationships that are formed and the moments that are shared will no doubt create memories that last a lifetime. Traveling provides student-athletes with the opportunity to make new friends and exposes them to other cultures, food, music, and traditions. As a coach, you can have a tremendous influence on the overall success of your team's travel experiences by talking with your athletes about appreciating and respecting the differences in people and their cultures, observing what they have in common, and truly staying in the moment while enjoying their surroundings.

CHAPTER 6 TRAINING YOUR ATHLETES

The fitness demands required to play a 90-minute game of soccer can be overwhelming for many athletes. Some athletes will be fairly fit and have the confidence to endure the conditioning they will face. Some athletes begin the season out of shape and struggle to get through the first few weeks. Others allow the psychological side of fitness to wear them down even though they may be fit enough to endure. Ultimately, because being fit makes everything else about the game easier, your job is to convince your athletes to accept responsibility for their fitness. Show them that they are in control and capable of becoming fit and staying fit. With a solid fitness base, your players will be confident that they have outworked their opponents in their preparation. Above all, once an athlete experiences the rewards of being fit, she will typically develop lifelong fitness habits.

To be successful as an individual and a team player, an athlete's training must be a combination of the physical and technical side of the game and the psychological and mental side of training. When an athlete practices a healthy lifestyle and has had proper mental preparation, she is more likely to experience a strong physical and technical game.

PHYSICAL TRAINING

Because of the various movements and types of running needed as soccer players, your athletes need to train both aerobically (creating stamina, or staying power) and anaerobically (for the shorter, more explosive aspects of the game). When planning training for your athletes, consider the primary physical components of a soccer conditioning program: flexibility, strength, power, endurance, agility, and speed.

Note: Teach only what you know, and recruit experts in the field to introduce areas that may not be your strength. For example, you may want to contact a strength and conditioning coach to outline a soccer-specific fitness program incorporating strength training, or a running coach to instruct your athletes on proper running mechanics when trying to improve their speed.

Flexibility

Flexibility defines the range of motion in a joint. A certain amount of flexibility is necessary to accomplish soccer-specific moves such as side volleys and throw-ins. Soccer players' quads

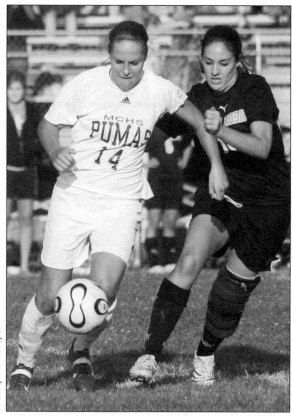

Courtesy of Chris Taylor

Self-discipline is a key component to the success of physically conditioned athletes.

and hamstrings can often be very tight as a result of the demands of the sport, so good flexibility will also help your athletes prevent injuries. It is important to incorporate a good stretching routine as part of a thorough warm-up. Following are a few flexibility exercises that you can use with your team:

• *Standing hamstring (hamstrings, calves, lower back, gluteus).* With your legs straight (do not lock your knees), spread them wider than your shoulders. Keeping your head in line with your upper body, reach with both hands to your right foot, then between your legs, and then to your left foot. Hold each stretch for 20 seconds or more.

• *Seated hamstring (hamstrings, lower back, calves).* Sit with your legs spread wide. Reach with your arms extended toward your left foot, then to the center, then toward your right foot. Hold each stretch for 20 seconds or more.

• *Sit and reach (hamstrings, gluteus, lower back).* While sitting, bend your left knee and

place your foot on the floor; the right leg extends straight out. Reach with both arms, one hand on top of the other, toward your outstretched foot. Hold the stretch for 20 seconds ore more and repeat on the other side.

• *Butt kicks (hamstrings and calves).* While jogging, quickly lift your heels to your gluteus. Keep your body upright; arm action is the same as when running.

Strength

Strength is the ability of the muscles to overcome resistance. Like flexibility, strength helps in injury prevention and endurance. Soccer players use strength in many ways, such as jumping to win balls in the air and keeping opponents off the ball while shielding with their bodies.

A common misconception is that strength training makes soccer players too slow or bulky. With proper planning, strength training will benefit your players and improve their performance, while helping to reduce the risk of injury. Before choosing the type of strength training to do with your athletes, first determine their needs based on their current fitness levels and the positions they play. Then look at the facilities available with regard to weight equipment.

Throughout the off-season, your athletes should focus on total conditioning. They should try to maintain a four- or five-day-a-week program with a focus on strength and power. During this time they are still working on flexibility, speed improvement, aerobic conditioning, and playing soccer. During the preseason, time spent on training outside the game decreases. Players now focus on being physically ready for the season and improving their skills as well as getting as many touches on the ball as possible. Strength training can now shift to approximately three days a week.

Following are a few exercises that you can use with your team to develop strength during the off-season and the preseason:

• *Leg press (quadriceps and hamstrings).* Place your feet approximately shoulder-width apart on the leg press surface. Lower the weight until your knees are bent at 90 degrees and then press to the starting position by extending your legs (do not lock the knees). Vary the workout by changing the position of your feet on the surface; for example, toes pointed in or out.

• *Bench press (anterior deltoids, triceps, pectoralis major).* Lie on a flat bench and grip the bar wider than shoulder width. Lower the bar until it is almost touching the sternum area; then press back to the starting position.

• *Barbell curl (biceps).* Start with your arms down at your sides. Grip the barbell with your palms up. Place your hands on the bar with a grip slightly wider than your hips. Keep your elbows near your sides. Bending at the elbows, raise the weight to shoulder height; then lower the weight and repeat.

• *Squats (quadriceps, gluteus, upper hamstrings, spinal erectors).* While standing, place a bar across the back of your neck and trapezius muscles (shoulders); your feet should be shoulder-width apart. While keeping your back straight, bend at the knees until the knee joints are approximately 90 degrees, and then extend back up to the starting position.

During the season, your athletes' strength-training regimen should focus on lifting lighter loads to maintain the strength they developed in the off-season and preseason. The emphasis is now placed on skills training and game preparation. You may benefit from having a strength and conditioning coach come in and work with your athletes to develop an appropriate strength-training program to incorporate into your practices approximately twice a week.

When most of us think of strength training, we think of lifting weights, but many programs do not have the use of weight rooms or weights during the season. Don't let this be a reason to ignore the importance of strength training. Here are some ways to gain strength without weights or other costly equipment:

• Sit-ups and push-ups on mats in the gym
• One-legged or two-legged jumps on the track or on stadium stairs
• V jumps or tuck jumps on the field
• Wall sits (like sitting in a chair only against a wall) in the hallway
• Leg lunges
• Plank position, resting on the toes and forearoms and keeping the body straight and lifted off the ground

Power

Power is the combination of speed and strength. Developing a good strength base is key for increasing power. Soccer players rely on power to sprint, jump, dive, and change direction quickly.

There are various ways to improve power. In addition to strength training, athletes can participate in plyometrics, which are exercises that combine speed and strength. Regardless of when the training begins, however, athletes should not do more than two plyometric drills per week. During the season the number of repetitions or types of drills can change, but the frequency should stay the same or lessen. Also, athletes should not do plyometrics on days when they have heavy cardiorespiratory or weight-training sessions. When planning plyometric sessions, start with basic movements that begin with two feet. As strength and power increase, add one-legged movements.

Following are a few plyometric exercises that that you can use with your team to develop power:

• Two-legged lateral hops over a ball
• Two-legged front and back hops over a ball
• Two-legged hops on bleacher steps
• One-legged, in-place, vertical jumps
• One-legged side-to-side jumps
• One-legged hops on bleacher steps

Endurance

Endurance is the ability to exert the body through aerobic and anaerobic exercise for extended periods of time. Endurance training is one of the most important elements of your conditioning program because soccer players do high-level running stints (requiring endurance and speed) with little or no rest between them. During a game, your athletes must be able to change speed and direction, jump, tackle, and strike a ball all while being pushed and shoved by opponents.

You should have a basic understanding of aerobic and anaerobic conditioning to prepare your athletes properly. The greater the player's aerobic capacity, the more ground she can cover during a game. In addition, improving her endurance and anaerobic capacity will increase the number of sprints she can complete in a game.

Aerobic capacity is the ability to use oxygen during exercise. This energy system is used in the periods between sprinting or fast, continuous movement; it is used more for endurance and less intense activity. Your soccer players need a good aerobic base because it is the building block for speed, endurance, and the ability to change pace repeatedly. During the season, limit longer runs for aerobic training because your girls are receiving it in the training drills and games. Off-season, they can run up to 30 minutes, approximately three times a week. This is a good time for your athletes to cross-train and build their aerobic foundation with other activities such as swimming, cycling, stair climbing, and using a treadmill.

Anaerobic capacity is the ability to perform repetitive, intense activity with little or no rest, without oxygen. This energy system produces fatigue in a short time (approximately two minutes). In this type of training the heart and muscles do not get the oxygen they need to function at that speed, so an athlete has to slow down, at which time her aerobic system takes over.

The most effective way to train for anaerobic fitness is through interval training. Sessions that incorporate high-intensity workouts with rest periods, producing gamelike situations, train your athletes to play longer and perform at a higher work rate. Vary the distance, time, sets, and repetitions as well as the rest intervals to incorporate interval training. There is no magic number or distance that creates the best results for your team. Try a variety of drills and see which ones work best with your players' fitness levels.

During the season, particularly if you have games twice a week, one intense anaerobic session should be enough. During the off-season, athletes should train for endurance four or five days a week. During the preseason, they should drop down to two or three sessions. By combining both aerobic and anaerobic components in your conditioning program, you will help your athletes achieve greater endurance levels while gaining and maintaining the ability to maintain speeds for longer periods of time, change pace and direction quickly, perform technical skills with less fatigue, and maintain concentration levels for longer periods of time.

Following are a few activities you can use with your players to help them develop endurance:

• *Fartlek training*. Fartlek training requires continuous exercise with intervals of speed followed by slower exercise for recovery. Vary the distance, repetition, and rest intervals for a variety in training. This training improves both anaerobic and aerobic fitness.

• *300-yard shuttles*. Place several cones 25 yards from the athletes' starting line. Athletes must sprint a total of 300 yards by sprinting out to the cones and back six times. They should recover fully before repeating the sprint. Depending on the fitness level of your team, you can set a time they must complete the 300 yards in, vary the sets, or change the recovery time.

• *2v2 + 1 possession*. Divide players into groups of five. Two players are attackers, two are defenders, and the fifth player wears a vest and is always on the team with possession. Mark an area of approximately 12 by 15 yards. Attackers start with the ball and try to maintain possession. The defenders try to steal the ball and gain possession. The defenders also get to start with the ball if it goes out of bounds. Each drill lasts two minutes. Make sure the floating player rotates, because her position can be very physically demanding.

Agility

Agility is the ability to start, stop, and change speed and direction quickly. In soccer, situations develop so fast that the athlete must be able to make quick decisions and act on them immediately; she has no time to think them through. Agility in soccer requires the athlete to not only change direction at top speed, but also do it while dribbling, passing, and receiving the ball. To have good agility, athletes must have good endurance, speed, strength, balance, and coordination. The changing environment in soccer requires that your athletes practice quick decision making.

Agility training can be done by performing coordination and agility drills in gamelike situations. Athletes who improve their agility improve their soccer skills and game performance.

Agility drills can be practiced year round—two or three times a week in the off-season and once or twice a week in the preseason. Make the time during the season to incorporate agility training at least once a week. Agility training not only helps your athletes get to the ball faster and stop and accelerate quicker, but also helps prevent injuries by improving body control through properly trained movement mechanics.

Following are a few exercises that you can use with your team to develop agility:

• *Lateral shuffle.* Athletes shuffle between cones placed 5 to 10 yards apart. The number of repetitions and sets depends on your objectives or time constraints. Do not allow the girls to let their feet cross over during the shuffle.

• *Sprint forward and backward.* Place cones 5 to 10 yards apart. Athletes sprint forward, then quickly backpedal. Athletes should use only a few steps to quickly transition from one movement to the next. Repetitions and sets depend on your objectives and time constraints.

• *Four corners.* Form a square with cones placed 5 to 10 yards apart. Athletes take turns starting at one cone, sprinting to the next cone, using a lateral shuffle (no crossover) to the next, and backpedaling to the next. They finish with a lateral shuffle to the last cone. When they reach the starting cone, they repeat in the opposite direction. Shorter rest periods between sets will improve their conditioning in addition to their agility. Change the size of the square to emphasize endurance or speed.

Speed

Speed is a combination of reaction time and movement time. Speed in soccer requires a lot more than just running fast. Soccer speed is the ability to accelerate quickly, react quickly, change direction quickly, produce bursts of fast running, anticipate, and move with the ball all while maintaining maximum speed. Players with speed can have a huge impact on a game. Defenses worry about attacking players with speed. Teams with speed typically increase their scoring opportunities because their players can get in the attacking third more often. With speed the game plan changes significantly. Most coaches agree that speed is a genetic factor,

but with commitment, athletes can improve their speed.

When training your athletes for speed, make sure they are properly warmed up and using proper running technique. Improving running form is something athletes must do in the off-season to correct flaws that are slowing them down. During the season, it is difficult to find the time to spend on running mechanics. You can help your players during their speed workouts by reviewing basic concepts of stride length and frequency as well as proper arm swing. Speed work should be done at the beginning of practice when players are fresh. Because speed work requires explosive movement, injuries can happen easily if athletes are tired.

As mentioned, during the off-season athletes should work on speed improvement by focusing on proper running technique. During the preseason athletes should be working on various sprint intervals approximately three times a week. During the season, sprint workouts should be designed around game schedules and limited to once or twice a week.

Following are a few activities that you can use with your team to develop speed:

• *Sprint ladder.* Athletes are lined up on the end line from fastest to slowest. Athletes sprint from the end line to sets of cones placed 20, 40, 60, and 80 yards away. The number of sprints at each distance will depend on your objectives and team fitness level. Players start by sprinting to the 20-yard cone on command. Each player is trying to "move up the ladder" by beating her teammate to the left. If she beats her, the two switch spots. The objective is to move as far left to the sideline as possible by beating the player on the left at each sprint interval. Players can move only one spot at a time. Give them time for a full recovery after each sprint.

• *25-yard shuttles.* Place cones every 5 yards up to 25 yards total. Athletes sprint to the first cone and back, second cone and back, and continue until the last cone. Athletes should turn sharply at each cone and rotate, pushing off with a different foot each time. Give a time that the shuttle must be completed in, and vary the recovery time.

• *Technical speed figure eights.* Athletes dribble in a figure-eight pattern. They should use the inside of both feet for six figure eights, then switch to using the outside of both feet for six more.

PSYCHOLOGICAL TRAINING

The physical and psychological sides of soccer go hand in hand. A major part of becoming fit is mental—and that's where a lot of girls struggle. Being willing to commit to the physical discomfort and fatigue that comes from conditioning is a psychological endeavor. When an athlete has conquered the physical side of her sport and can concentrate on playing, she has acquired mental and emotional strength and confidence.

How many of your players have been in games or training sessions in which everything goes right? From their first touch or shot, they can tell it's going to be a good performance. But when you ask them what they did to achieve such an amazing performance, most athletes cannot explain it. They will agree, however, that their emotional or mental state was a key factor. Being mentally prepared for training or a game requires practice and is as important as physical training and learning the techniques and tactics of the sport.

Many poor performances are not a result of physical or technical shortcomings, but rather of underlying mental, emotional, or lifestyle issues. The athletes who perform at the top of their games know the importance of the mental side of the game. They choose to have a positive winning attitude, and with that comes confidence. Having the ability to recover from mistakes or the loss of an important game is a key characteristic of confidence. The confident athlete knows that being confident is an everyday decision; she takes ownership of her setbacks and knows that with the right attitude things will be fine.

Many things can boost players' confidence. One is experience—knowing they can handle a situation because they have experienced it before and know what to expect. Positive self-talk is another way players can boost their confidence. Players who understand the importance of psychological training and value it find that

Learning to trust your intuition and staying true to yourself allows athletes to develop the inner strength to realize their potential.

they have more self-control. They see problems as challenges, and they enjoy the game more.

Psychological skills, such as goal setting, mental imagery, and affirmations, can enhance athletes' performances, as discussed in previous chapters. One of the greatest things athletes can learn through mental preparation is that they are in control of their responses to circumstances surrounding them. Despite low or frustrating moments, athletes can learn to write their own scripts for the game and have solid performances regardless of previous mistakes.

Athletes who have not practiced or learned psychological skills tend to stay focused on mistakes, resulting in poor performance and a lack of self-confidence. As coaches, we understand that performance and confidence are very much related. An athlete who has learned to control her response to her performance using mental imagery and affirmations has the ability to take a mistake and turn it into a learning experience, to turn a negative into a positive. Help your athletes understand that their psychological state is a part of everything they do—how they train, their mental toughness, and their ability to correct mistakes and play with confidence.

Teaching your athletes the power of mental imagery and affirmations is not easy, but don't give up. With a little maturity and leadership from older teammates, your athletes will see these skills as powerful tools that aid their performance. Just like tactical or technical skills, psychological skills require practice, repetition, and positive reinforcement from the coaching staff.

Mental Imagery

Mental imagery—or visualization—is an important part of athletes' psychological training. It requires that they use their senses to create experiences in their minds. They imagine themselves playing soccer and "see" plays develop in their minds. The more details they can include in their images, the more vivid their visualizations will be. Have your players see, hear, feel, and smell the environment. They should include the weather and the physical surroundings in their images. The more relaxed they are, the more focused their visualizations will be.

When done correctly, the process of visualization is so powerful that the central nervous system cannot distinguish between the image and the athlete actually performing the skill. Visualizing an action becomes another form of practice. Once the image becomes part of a player's memory, she can use it when she faces a similar situation in a game. The more your athletes practice visualization, the better they become at creating powerful images. This type of training has tremendous benefits for athletes who use it consistently. However, like any form of training, athletes will only realize the benefits if they practice it on a regular basis. This should not be a one-time training method.

To help players get the most out of their visualizations, create a quiet, calm, and peaceful atmosphere in which they can focus on the process. Have them take several slow, deep breaths, clearing their minds and relaxing their entire bodies. Then have them visualize their ideal performance and remind them to use all of their senses. They should always visualize positive actions, be specific, include details, stay calm and relaxed, and most important, be patient. Benefits will come if they are consistent with their practice.

Players who use visualizations successfully benefit in several ways: They improve relaxation and learn how to block out distractions, they build self-confidence because they see their skills in a positive light, and they learn self-control and how to manage their emotions. Most important, they learn the significance of the body–mind connection and realize that their thoughts play an important part in their search for consistent peak performance.

Affirmations

Affirmations are statements that keep athletes on track. They are strong, positive, and concise phrases that confirm goals or objectives. Affirmations are another way to create possibilities and opportunities by changing negative thoughts into positive reinforcements. The words an athlete uses can become her reality.

Give your athletes the following guidelines for creating affirmations:

• *Keep affirmations short and simple.* The affirmation "I improve with every move" is preferable to "I will improve every time I move to receive or pass the ball." Affirmations that are short and concise are easier to remember, encouraging athletes to use them on a regular basis. A long, detailed affirmation would require the athlete to memorize it as opposed to feeling it and using it in a positive way.

• *Focus on what you want, not on what you don't want.* Most athletes have to be reminded to focus on what they want, not on what they do not want. For example, instead of saying, "I don't want this shot to go up the middle directly to the goalkeeper," the athlete should say, "My shot will be to the left/right of the goalkeeper and in the back of the net." Negative thoughts and words create anxiety and self-doubt, two things that severely hinder performance. Because thoughts and words create reality, your athletes should focus on positive statements.

CHAPTER 7
CONDUCTING PRACTICES

We all want our athletes to learn how to maintain their focus and intensity in practice. We want them to show up each day with energy and enthusiasm, understanding that the way they train will translate into the way they compete. By preparing productive daily practice plans, you can help this happen on a regular basis.

Although preparing daily practice plans can be time consuming, the advantages far outweigh the disadvantages. Practice plans help you stay organized throughout the season and provide a blueprint for teaching the necessary technical and tactical skills. Thoroughly planned training sessions make better use of practice time, space, and equipment. Athletes typically learn more, stay more focused and engaged, and have more fun when practices are well planned. In addition, the transitions between practice components are smoother. You will find your athletes saying, "Practice is over?" rather than, "What time is it?"

CREATING PRACTICE PLANS

Creating practice plans is the next step after you've developed the goals and plans for the season. To do this, break your season down first by month and then by the day.

Monthly Practice Plans

If you are new to coaching or do not consider yourself an organized person, creating a monthly practice plan is a great way to prepare for your season's practices. However, keep in mind that monthly plans are merely outlines for practice sessions because, as you know, much can change in four weeks. You don't want to spend a lot of time and energy focusing on a situation that may no longer be an issue several weeks down the road. Just as you want your athletes to perform "in the moment" without worrying about yesterday's mistakes or what tomorrow will bring, so too should you regard your planning for training. Use your monthly plan mainly as a guide to keep you on track with your seasonal plans and objectives.

To create a monthly practice plan, start with a blank monthly calendar and fill in the dates for games and then training sessions. Take time to think about the emphasis, or main objective, of each practice for each month of the season and fill these in on the calendar, as shown in figure 7.1. When creating your objectives, consider your players' needs based on preseason evaluations as well their learning styles. Although your practice pace, or intensity level, will remain steady from week to week, your strategies will change for various opponents. Prior to competing against tougher teams, you may

Monthly Practice Plan

September						
Sun	Mon	Tue	Wed	Thu	Fri	Sat
	1 **Emphasis**: Fitness and conditioning	2 **Emphasis**: Formation and attacking shape	3 **Emphasis**: Defensive style and tendencies	4 Scrimmage	5 Preseason game	6 No training
7 No training	8 **Emphasis**: Fitness and conditioning	9 **Emphasis**: Passing and transitions	10 Game day	11 **Emphasis**: Finishing and organizing set plays	12 Game day	13 Strength training circuit work
14 No training	15 **Emphasis**: Fitness and conditioning	16 **Emphasis**: Dribbling and attacking	17 Game day	18 **Emphasis**: Defensive pressure, turning, and shooting	19 Game day	20 No training
21 No training	22 **Emphasis**: Fitness and conditioning	23 **Emphasis**: Possession and shape	24 Game day	25 **Emphasis**: Shooting and finishing	26 Game day	27 Strength training circuit work
28 No training	29 **Emphasis**: Fitness and conditioning	30 **Emphasis**: Defensive shape and communication				

Figure 7.1

want to design your practices around playing those teams.

Daily Practice Plans

Once you have created a monthly plan, you are ready to create daily plans to help you manage your practice time and remain focused on your goals. Keep in mind that, like monthly plans, daily plans may need to be adjusted—this time, based on your next opponent or the strengths and weaknesses exposed in previous games. The time you spend practicing with your team is valuable, and you don't want to waste it; however, you don't want to be so rigid in following your daily schedule that you ignore the rhythm and energy of your athletes. Also, try not to plan too far ahead or create too many detailed practices in advance. You'll need to remain flexible and be willing to adjust to changing circumstances as the season progresses. The one constant is that a season rarely goes as predicted; injuries happen and players learn differently and at different paces. You'll also be dealing with weather conditions, facility problems, and many more unforeseen factors. Your intention should be to stay focused on your seasonal goals while remaining flexible in your day-to-day sessions.

Following are descriptions of the components of a practice, as shown in figure 7.2:

• *Prepractice meeting.* Take time to meet with your athletes during the first 5 to 10 minutes of practice, prior to the warm-up. This is the time to review your practice plan for the day, review the previous day's game, or make important team-related announcements.

• *Warm-up.* Next, your players will need a proper warm-up with various running and stretching routines. In the beginning of the season, you will need to run the warm-up yourself. As the season progresses, your team captains can take over this responsibility. Consider supplementing your warm-up with an activity that will quickly transition the team into the main session of the practice.

• *Main session.* The main session of the practice focuses on the skill emphasized in your season plan. At this time you introduce the main topic or focus for practice. For example, if your emphasis is on dribbling, break down the dribbling technique you're looking for and give

your athletes time to practice it before using it in an activity or gamelike situation.

• *Activities.* Each practice should include two or three activities that progress from simple to complex. The focus of this part of the practice is either technical or tactical training, and it requires the athletes' complete focus. This portion should usually consume about 50 to 60 percent of your practice time, depending on the experience of your team. The activities should also emphasize what the players just learned in the main session; they give you an opportunity to watch your athletes put what they've just learned into a game situation. Demand game-day pace and intensity. You can stop play and make corrections while choreographing players' movement and passing patterns, but try not to overdo the interruptions. Let the players play. This is also a good time to take notes and evaluate players' progress.

• *Cool-down.* The cool-down should take place during the last 5 to 10 minutes of practice and should focus on slow runs and stretching. Your captains can incorporate push-up and sit-up routines if they were not done in the other portions of your training.

• *Postpractice meeting.* The postpractice meeting is used for any closing remarks about the day's practice or any brief reminders for the following day. Also, use this time to have the players pick up and put away equipment. Finally, before everyone leaves for the day, perform the team cheer.

RUNNING PRACTICES

Naturally, you expect your athletes to show up to practice focused, energetic, and ready to learn. But, let's face it, getting together five or six days a week for three months straight can get tedious. You can help your players prepare for practice so that they get the most out of their training session, and teach them how to practice with a purpose.

Preparing Players for Practice

To achieve the high level of focus and concentration that most coaches demand, players

Daily Practice Plan

Emphasis: *Dribbling*

Objective: *To develop players' ability to take on opponents, improve dribbling maneuvers, and attack with speed*

Date: *September 16, 2008*

Practice time: *3:30 p.m.*

Special equipment: *Mini-goals, flags (12), cones*

	Description	Notes
3:30-3:40	Prepractice meeting and comments	• No bus for tomorrow's game; confirm carpools. • Check on sizes for sweatshirt order. • Team dinner Thursday night at Hayley's. • Folders—write out three affirmations for Thursday.
3:40-3:55	Warm-up	• Ball control and agility series • Stretch routine • Starting on a corner of the field and covering the penalty boxes and circumference of the field, two players alternate sprinting then jogging at each new line.
3:55-4:15	Main session: Dribbling	Place two cones 1 yard apart, or use mini-goals if available. Place another set of cones 1 yard apart and 25 to 30 yards away. Two or three players are lined up behind each set of mini-goals or cones; the ball starts on either side. A ball is played to the first player in line. The player sends the ball and then follows her pass, trying to stop the receiving player from dribbling past her and scoring by dribbling the ball through the opposite goal. Players take each other on for one to two minutes until you end the round. The next two players continue the drill. Players waiting for their turns stretch and collect loose balls.
4:15-4:30	Activity: Bogies	Divide your team into three groups of attackers, midfielders, and defenders. Attackers and defenders line up at the same goal but on opposite goalposts facing the field. Midfielders bring all the balls to the middle of the field. Play begins when an attacker checks to the midfield with an angled run. The first midfielder plays a ball to the checking attacker, and the first defender releases to challenge, setting up a 1v1 situation. The passing midfielder moves to support the attacker, giving the tactical support for a 2v1. Attackers pass to midfielders only if they cannot beat the defender and go to goal. If the attacker passes to the midfielder, a second defender is released, creating a 2v2 situation. Play continues with this progression until a 3v3 situation develops, if necessary.

4:30-4:50	Activity: 2v2 through gates	Players are organized in two or three groups with six to eight in each group. Use cones to create a 15-square-yard grid for each group and disperse five or six mini-goals throughout the grid. Players partner up and go 2v2 within the grid, trying to score as many goals as possible by dribbling through the mini-goals. They can score by dribbling through the cones in any direction while trying to maintain possession with their partners. Players keep track of their own points. Each round lasts one to two minutes. The two athletes with the most points from each grid advance to a championship round. Players can play single or double elimination.
4:50-5:10	Activity: 5v5 to big goals	Use an area half the size of your soccer field with standard-size goals set up on each of the sidelines between the end line and midfield line. Organize players in groups of five. While two teams play, the other one or two teams do strength training exercises, juggling, or other ball-skill related drills. If you have enough goals, the other two teams can play on the other half of the field. Players scrimmage for a designated time (five to eight minutes) and follow the theme you call out. If you say, "Change the point of attack," then the team in possession cannot score until it has changed the point of attack at least once. Each time you call a new theme, players must respond and perform the theme before shooting on goal.
5:10-5:20	Cool-down	• Abdominal routine with push-ups • Stretching • Ball massages
5:20-5:30	Postpractice meeting and comments	• Closing remarks • Equipment cleanup • Team cheer

Figure 7.2

need to learn how to live balanced lives and let go of problems. They also need to learn to appreciate the moment and enjoy working with their teammates regardless of the kind of day they've had.

In my program, during the 10- to 15-minute warm-up, the players run and stretch while talking about their day, checking in with the coaches, and telling funny stories. Those little moments of sharing and learning about each other make us closer as a team and remind us of how much we have in common and how much fun we have in each other's company. As an off-campus coach, I enjoy the fact that they want to laugh about and share their day with me. The day that minutes on the clock become more important than allowing relationships to blossom is the day I stop coaching! If you add it all up—and believe me, some coaches do—I may lose an hour a week of tactical training as a result of giving my girls that time to socialize. What I gain, though, is a team full of sisters who know each other's life stories and will lay it on the line for each other when the time comes.

Changing your team's training environment can refresh and invigorate their outlook and attitude toward conditioning.

If You Really Knew Me...

One team-building activity that I do every year is called If You Really Know Me. Typically, at the end of a hard training session each week, I bring a healthy snack for the players to share, and they sit in a circle while each player takes a turn finishing the sentence, *If you really knew me* .... Because this activity is usually a very emotional one, it should not be rushed. There are no limits to what girls can decide to share with each other, and there is an understanding that this is personal information that they should not share with anyone outside the team. Sometimes a girl's sentence will be as simple as "If you really knew me, you'd know that my favorite food is spaghetti." Usually it is something far more personal.

During this activity, players begin to trust each other as teammates and know that if they show their vulnerable side they will not be ridiculed. Some players have a hard time opening up; others are ready and willing to share their stories. However, most players come around once they see their teammates being honest with them. When athletes trust enough to share personal experiences with each other, they begin to develop a sense of loyalty to the team. Building emotional bonds allows them to get through the most difficult times.

Quite often the fresh air and endorphins released during the physical exercise exerted during practice are exactly what your players need to turn a bad day into a better day. Talk with the girls about taking care of problems outside of soccer and give them the tools necessary to let these problems go once they step onto the field. One way to support them in this process is to use your prepractice meeting to pair the girls up to talk with each other about anything that is bothering them. Give them a few minutes to share with each other, and then bring them back into the larger group and have each girl share her teammate's problem with the team if necessary. She starts off by saying, "If you really knew [*player's name*], then you'd know that she is dealing with [*player's problem*]." Sharing their problems in this way helps the girls let their teammates know what they're going through without getting too emotional about the situation. This is not a question-and-answer period, but rather a time to just listen and really hear what their teammates are going through. Under the right guidance, at the right time, this can be a very powerful experience for your athletes.

Practicing With a Purpose

It takes discipline to practice with purpose. As a coach, you can emphasize "training on the edge" and give them a vision of what that looks like. At the beginning of the season, ask your players, "What does playing with intensity look like in this sport?" and have them respond by writing out their visions. Collect and discuss the visions as a team so they have a clear picture of what training for excellence looks like. Many athletes use the term *training with intensity,* but what does that really mean to them? Once they are forced to "see it and say it," then they can be held accountable for it. A field player's vision might be to "work hard on both sides of the ball," and a goalkeeper may strive to "verbally communicate specific instructions to the backline."

Remind your athletes that the way they train in practice is the way they will play in the game. When it comes to game time, they rely totally on recall. You can give the best pregame motivational speech you've ever given, but that will take them only so far. Recall comes from the things you've engrained in them at practice and the habits they have developed. Training with intensity is about developing those habits.

Ongoing, clear communication is essential for a healthy relationship between players and coaches. If you are clear and concise about your expectations of your athletes, then they will show up prepared to meet those expectations or to suffer the consequences.

Our players understand that practice begins at 3:30. This starting time is firm regardless of whether we are starting with a meeting or going directly into the warm-up. Players are excused only if they have informed me in advance about an appointment, tutoring, or an injury that may need to be taken care of in the training room (by either me or an assistant coach). Our athletes are out of school at 3:05; with practice beginning at 3:30, they don't have a lot of time to waste. After getting out of class, going to their lockers or cars to get their practice gear, and making their way to the team room, they have only 15 minutes to get ready and be out on the field. With a locker room full of girls getting ready for the other fall sports (cross country, volleyball, tennis), that's not a lot of time.

If a player has to miss a practice completely, she must call my cell phone or office and let me know in advance. If she neglects to call and misses a session, she meets with me and I explain that if it happens again, she will no longer be a member of the team. Fortunately, we've never had to go past that initial warning.

Part III

COACHING SKILLS

CHAPTER 8 DRIBBLING

Dribbling in soccer is the ability to control the ball with the feet while moving around the field. The player with that "something special" makes the crowd sit up with anticipation when she gets the ball at her feet. These players are the main reasons stadiums fill seats. Unfortunately, fewer players these days have the technical and creative ability to take on opponents while having complete control over their bodies and the ball. Without proper technical training on a consistent basis, few soccer players can rise above the average level of play. Developing these technical abilities is key to competitive soccer. Unless training programs encourage individual attacking techniques, particularly at an early age, we will begin to see fewer of these "personality players."

When working on developing your athletes' dribbling skills, encourage them to find and develop their own strengths and styles. You need to teach proper mechanics, but once your players have mastered those, allow them to explore their own creativity and discover what works best for them. Some players use a lot of sharp cuts while continually twisting their defenders. Others are more direct, dribbling at the opponent using changes of pace and acceleration moves. You can help your athletes develop their own dribbling styles by allowing them the freedom to be creative with the ball.

As players get older, however, the type of dribbling they focus on usually becomes more about their positions on the field. Defenders, for example, are often forced to "speed dribble" to get out of trouble quickly and get the ball out of their defensive third. All players need to spend time developing skills in the various types of dribbling to have the confidence to try different positions. Players who learn to dribble effectively enhance their confidence in any situation.

TYPES OF DRIBBLING

Before learning about dribbling technique and specific dribbling maneuvers, you should first recognize the three types of dribbling used in a soccer game based on the situation: dribbling to maintain possession, dribbling to beat an opponent, and dribbling with speed.

Dribbling to Maintain Possession

Players who excel at dribbling to maintain possession can control the game by setting up and executing specific attacks. In soccer, attacking plays are often designed because a specific player has a strong ability to hold on to the ball and penetrate into space for a successful shot, pass, or cross. For example, midfielders who are able to hold on to the ball while under pressure can give their teammates time to make supporting runs. Likewise, forwards who have the ability to hold the ball can give their teammates time to move into supporting positions for attacking combinations.

Although dribbling skills are a major factor in your team's attacking abilities, too much dribbling can inadvertently hurt your team's efforts to maintain possession of the ball. Players must find the balance between successful dribbling and passing. Excessive dribbling in the defensive third of the field is dangerous and can lead to a scoring opportunity for the opponent, whereas dribbling in the attacking third can lead to a scoring opportunity for one's own team. Losing the ball in the attacking third is not as costly as losing it in one's own defensive third.

Dribbling to Beat an Opponent

Dribbling to beat an opponent involves running with the ball to get past an opponent in order to penetrate empty space, take a shot on goal, or buy time for teammates to make runs for better field positions from which to receive the ball. This type of dribbling is most often used in the middle or attacking third of the field, where midfielders and forwards can run with pace at the opponent because they have space to work with. Forwards who can outrun opponents can set themselves up for a final pass to a teammate or create enough space for their own shot on goal.

Dribbling With Speed

Dribbling with speed is used on transition and to counterattack the opponents before they can get organized behind the ball. Depending on time and space, players can push the ball ahead of themselves to accelerate into a dribble on the run, which is typically called a speed dribble. Flank (wide) players need to get plenty of practice in speed dribbling because they often have more space to work with. Flank players with good speed dribbling techniques create opportunities to cut inside and go directly to goal or

to the end line for an early cross that can catch the defense out of position.

DRIBBLING TECHNIQUE

Athletes must learn proper dribbling techniques before they can successfully take on opponents. Players can use various foot surfaces to give them more options while dribbling. Dribbling can be done with the inside, outside, instep, and sole of the foot.

Using the various foot surfaces, your athletes should practice changing direction and running with the ball at various speeds, while focusing on keeping the ball under control. Organize drills that force them to use both feet, keep their heads up while dribbling, and pay attention to what is going on around them. As they become more comfortable and confident with the ball, work on changes of pace and speed dribbling.

To be successful, athletes should keep their center of gravity low by leaning forward and bending slightly at the knees. They should focus on getting defenders off balance by attacking their front feet and changing pace while performing their moves. It helps to stay on the toes and be prepared to move laterally in either direction. Emphasize in training that in a game situation, they will have to decide which move to use right on the spot! Defenders will not give them time to think about their moves. Your athletes must learn how to be creative and understand that successful dribbling comes down to practice, timing, awareness, and experience.

Dribbling With the Inside of the Foot

Dribbling with the inside of the foot is the type of dribbling players typically use when first learning how to dribble. Using the inside of the foot is a natural movement that keeps the ball in line with the center of the body, making it easier for beginners to move the ball while running. This type of dribbling is not typically used for speed, so beginning athletes can learn by moving slower with the ball and taking lighter touches to keep it close. It is effective for cutting the ball back and forth against a defender, or for changing direction quickly.

Figure 8.1 Dribbling with the inside of the foot.

When dribbling with the inside of the foot, the player should be in a balanced stance, keeping her center of gravity low by bending slightly at the knees and waist and leaning her body in the direction of play. The player should keep her arms extended with a slight bend at the elbow to help maintain balance and to keep a distance between herself and an opponent. When contacting the ball, the player keeps her foot perpendicular to the ball and touches it lightly. She kicks through the center of the ball to control the direction and keep it close to her body (see figure 8.1). The foot is locked, and the toes are lifted. The player should also keep her head up and eyes focused on the field while she is dribbling the ball.

Dribbling With the Outside of the Foot

Dribbling with the outside of the foot allows a player to change direction and focus on attacking a defender's plant foot, keeping her off

balance. This type of dribbling is excellent for moving the ball at high speeds in addition to cutting the ball and changing direction. The player must stay balanced and light on her feet.

When dribbling with the outside of the foot, a player should be in a balanced stance and keep her center of gravity low by bending slightly at the knees and waist. The player should keep her arms extended with a slight bend at the elbow to help maintain balance and to keep a distance between herself and an opponent. When contacting the ball, she should use the top center of the outside of the foot to push the center of the ball. She should point the foot slightly downward with the ankle locked and the toes slightly lifted upward (see figure 8.2). In addition, at contact with the ball, the first touch should also be the first stride, allowing the athlete to build momentum quickly. Because this type of dribbling is usually associated with speed, the ball is pushed farther ahead into space (depending on the position of the opponent). Therefore, the athlete's stride is typically longer so she can stay closer to the ball.

Figure 8.2 Dribbling with the outside of the foot.

Dribbling With the Instep

Dribbling with the instep, or the top of the foot, allows a player to run at a defender at a higher speed because it is a natural forward motion. This technique allows a player to work on technical speed while nudging the ball forward and drawing in the defender to keep her off balance. Again, attacking the defender's front foot makes it difficult for her to recover as the player accelerates out of the move.

When dribbling with the instep, a player should be in a balanced stance and keep her center of gravity low by bending slightly at the knees and waist. The player should keep her arms extended with a slight bend at the elbow to help maintain balance and to keep a distance between herself and an opponent. When contacting the ball, the player keeps her foot in a vertical position, with the toe down, and uses the top of the foot to nudge the ball forward (see figure 8.3).

Figure 8.3 Dribbling with the instep.

DRIBBLING MANEUVERS

Shielding, cutting, pulling, and feinting are techniques used when dribbling and maintaining possession of the ball. Each requires a combination of balance and anticipation. Physical strength in both the legs and upper body are important as well, particularly when shielding the ball. It is the opponent's job to get the ball back, and most will do it by using their bodies to force the player with the ball off balance. Your athletes must learn how to stay strong on their feet and practice good balance skills. They need to learn how to be aggressive in holding on to the ball while taking control of the situation. They should not let the opponent push them off the ball.

Anticipating what the opponent will do can help your athletes make quick decisions about what to do with the ball. Learning how to anticipate takes practice and experience; it cannot necessarily be trained. However, you can encourage your athletes to think like the opponent and develop confidence in their abilities. Confident players believe they can hold on to the ball by using the following dribbling maneuvers combined with staying strong on the ball, maintaining their balance, keeping their heads up, and anticipating the opponents' moves.

Shielding

When dribbling to maintain possession, your player must shield—or protect—the ball from the opponent to make it easier to maintain possession. Shielding is most often used when players run out of room to dribble and are tightly marked, or when they simply cannot outrun a chasing opponent.

To shield, the player positions her body sideways between the ball and the opponent and keeps the ball on the foot farthest from the opponent. She must not be afraid to use her body to push the opponent away from the ball (see figure 8.4). The player should also extend the arm closest to the opponent to help maintain distance and should always strive to keep her head up to keep her eyes on the field. She must avoid turning her back to an incoming defender when shielding the ball. Holding on to the ball is difficult when a player can't see what

Figure 8.4 Using the body to shield the ball.

her opponent is doing. She should try to keep a shoulder pointed toward the defender when possible. The only time it is acceptable to turn her back is when she knows she has support behind her and can quickly play the ball back to a teammate.

Cutting

Your players also need to learn how to escape when an opponent closes in on them by cutting the ball, or spinning to move in a new direction. Attacking players who master cutting make it difficult for their opponents to defend against them.

To cut while moving the ball forward, the player points her toe down and pushes the ball with the inside or outside of the foot (see figure 8.5*a*). To cut when moving the ball laterally, the player should pull her toe up in most situations. If space is available, she should push the ball long and explode to stay with the ball, using the instep to follow through with the ball (see figure 8.5*b*).

Figure 8.5 Cutting when moving the ball forward (*a*) and laterally (*b*).

Once she cuts, the athlete can then perform several moves, three of which are listed here. In addition, you can incorporate these moves into a warm-up to work on quickness, or use them to teach explosiveness.

• *Cut inside-outside.* Cut the ball with the inside of one foot, and touch it forward with the outside of the opposite foot. Continue cutting inside-outside using both feet.

• *Cut inside-inside.* Cut the ball under the body with the inside of one foot, play it forward with the inside of the opposite foot, and repeat.

• *Cut outside-inside.* Cut the ball with the outside of one foot, and play it forward with the inside of the same foot. Rotate with both feet and repeat.

Pulling

When dribbling, the athlete can use pulling to bring the ball closer to her body and away from the opponent. Pulling is used in preparation for taking a player on with a dribbling move. To pull the ball, the player uses the sole of the foot and pulls the ball back toward her body to set up for the next move (see figure 8.6). This is a great technique to use when the opponent is in front of the athlete and closing in quickly.

Once a player pulls the ball back closer to her body, she can then perform one of several moves, two of which are listed here. In addition, you can incorporate these moves into a warm-up to work on quickness or use them to teach explosiveness.

• *Pull inside-outside.* Pull the ball back under the body with the sole of one foot, then touch it with the inside of the opposite foot, followed by the outside of the same foot. Imagine drawing a V on the ground. Rotate and repeat, and keep it going side to side.

• *Pull outside-outside.* Pull the ball with the sole of one foot, then touch it twice with the opposite foot. The second touch is a small preparing touch, whereas the third touch is a penetrating forward touch to blow past the opponent. Again, imagine drawing a V on the ground.

Figure 8.6 Pulling the ball away from the opponent.

Feinting

Feints are moves that rely on body fakes in one direction while taking the ball in the opposite direction. When players learn how and when to use a feint in various situations with particular moves, they become even more dangerous with the ball. An example of a feint is a *fake shot and push to the side* move, in which the player fakes as if she were going to take a shot (see figure 8.7*a*) and then takes the ball with the outside of the same foot and pushes it around the defender (see figure 8.7*b*).

DRIBBLING ACTIVITIES

Mastering dribbling and attacking skills gives players confidence with the ball and makes them capable of maintaining possession while controlling the tempo of the game. The difficulty for most coaches is finding the time to cover all aspects of the game in the short amount of time they have with athletes. The season is typically only a few months long, and you are training various ages and maturity levels as well as various skill levels. For this reason, technical training on the ball becomes even more important.

Figure 8.7 Feinting: faking a shot and pushing the ball with the outside of the same foot and around the defender.

For players to become technically solid with the ball, they have to spend time on their own to reinforce the necessary skills and develop confidence and creativity with the ball. You can encourage this habit of working on their own by insisting they get a ball and dribble while waiting for practice to start. Once they feel a little success in their dribbling abilities, they will become more committed to training. In short, players must understand that they must be strong individually to play strong collectively.

The following dribbling drills will teach your athletes when and how to execute the correct dribbling techniques in a variety of tactical situations while becoming more confident on the ball.

Figure Eights

Objectives Dribbling warm-up to develop change of pace using the inside and outside of the foot while making sharp turns and keeping the ball close.

Description Players work individually with a ball and two cones 6 yards apart. On your signal, starting at one cone, players dribble figure eights between the cones with explosive movements as they turn around one cone and accelerate to the next. Players follow your direc-

tives for dribbling with the inside of the foot, the outside of the foot, and a combination of inside, outside foot patterns. They should rotate using both the left and right feet and change the direction of travel after each round. Rounds last 30 to 60 seconds.

Attacking the Square

Objectives To develop the ability to take players on 1v1, gain confidence in their ability to maintain possession, and expand on their moves.

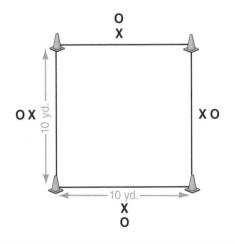

Figure 8.8 Attacking the Square.

Description   Groups of eight players are in 10-× 10-yard grids (see figure 8.8). Players are designated as four attackers (O) and four defenders (X). Each attacker has a ball. Defenders stand 5 yards from the outside of the grid lines; they cannot cross into the square. Attackers start 10 yards from the defenders. The attackers try to maintain possession and dribble the ball into the square, getting a point each time they are successful. Players play 60- to 90-second rounds. If the attacker gets in the square before time runs out, she can come back out and try again for another point. Attackers rotate clockwise on your signal, getting an opportunity to go against each of the four defenders. Attackers and defenders rotate after a full round. Keep track of points, and have a championship round with the top four players with the highest scores.

1v1 to Goal

Objectives   To develop the fundamentals of beating opponents in a 1v1 situation with game-like pace; also develops great communication opportunities between the goalkeeper and her defenders.

Description   Separate a team into offensive and defensive players. Set up two standard goals on the same end line, approximately 20 yards apart. Split defenders (X) and place them at all four goalposts. Place a goalkeeper (GK) in each goal. Split attackers (O) into two lines at the midline with balls. Place a cone 10 yards from the midfield, lined up in front of each goal. The first attacker in each line sprints to the cone in front of her and checks back to receive the ball played by the next person in line (see figure 8.9). As soon as the attacking player checks, one of the defenders releases with a verbal cue from her goalkeeper. Both the attacking and the defending player continue the 1v1 until a shot is taken or the defender clears the ball out of the area. Having both goals at the same end line creates a loud, chaotic environment and keeps the drill moving quickly at game pace. All players must remain focused and calm and learn how to finish under these circumstances.

Variations

- Attackers can be given specific instructions instead of reading the situation,

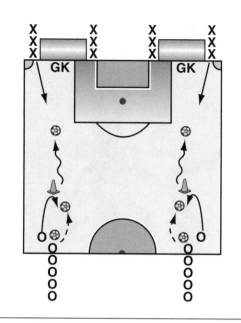

Figure 8.9   1 v 1 to Goal.

such as "turn and shoot" as soon as they receive the ball, or "take on the goalkeeper" instead of shooting.

- Attackers can start their runs from the flank.

- Defenders can take on specific tasks such as "do the opposite of what the goalkeeper says," or "don't release unless the goalkeeper uses your name."

Dribbling Breakaways

Objectives   To develop dribbling speed, improve reaction time, increase awareness of goalkeeper positioning, and improve decision making about what type of shot to take.

Description   Separate a team into offensive and defensive players. Split both into two groups and place a goalkeeper (GK) in the goal. One group of offensive (O) and one group of defensive (X) players line up side by side approximately 10 yards from the sideline (separated by cones or flags) and even with the tip of the center circle. The other group lines up the same way on the opposite side. A server (S), typically the coach, is in the center circle with the balls (see figure 8.10).

Starting on the left side, the first offensive player checks to the server while calling for the

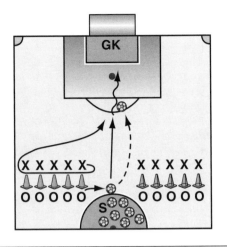

Figure 8.10 Dribbling Breakaways.

ball, but then quickly turns upfield to prepare to receive a ball played into the space near the top of the 18-yard box. As soon as the offensive player checks, the defender must run and touch the last flag in line before she can chase down the offense. With a trailing defender coming, the offensive player (dribbling at top speed) must decide whether to take on the goalkeeper in a 1v1 situation, chip her if she's way off her line, or take a shot depending on the goalkeeper's positioning. As soon as a shot is taken, the next group on the opposite side begins the pattern. The offensive player should have a big first touch to cover distance while looking up at the goalkeeper. If the goalkeeper is charging, the offensive player should chip it. If the goalkeeper is coming out slowly, the offensive player should go straight at her for a 1v1. If the goalkeeper is moving and off balance, the offensive player should shoot it low. Players should use body feints to get the goalkeeper off balance while dribbling with speed.

Variations
- Run the activity on both sides of the field for more action and less standing.
- Add a second defender and then release a second attacker.

CHAPTER 9
PASSING, RECEIVING, AND TURNING

Although it is exciting to watch players with exceptional dribbling skills, it is just as exciting to watch a team that moves the ball well with perfectly placed passes. When fans refer to a game as "pretty" or a team that plays "pretty soccer," they are typically referring to the way players consistently string quality passes together. Passing, receiving, and turning are grouped together because each pass should be received and controlled by a teammate. With good passing, receiving, and turning techniques, teams can control the tempo of the game while building efficient attacking strategies.

PASSING

In soccer, passing is how a team moves the ball from one player to another to advance the ball up the field and set up scoring opportunities. Passing the ball is one of the most important technical skills a player can master for several reasons: It allows a team to move the ball quickly up the field and maintain possession, it creates space by spreading out the players on the field, and it creates scoring opportunities. Players must learn how to pass the ball under pressure from opponents with limited time and space, and often while fatigued.

Good passing requires that players pass the ball at the right speed (pace), at the right moment (timing), and to the right spot (accuracy). Let's take a look at these a little more closely:

Pace

- The pass should be weighted properly, based on the situation (i.e., it should not be too hard or too soft).
- The pass should be at a speed that allows the receiving player to easily control and prepare the ball for the next move.

Timing

- Players must know when to target a teammate's foot and when to serve the ball into space so the teammate can receive it without breaking stride.
- Players must know when to send a driven ball that gets to the target quickly and when to send a flighted ball (in the air and usually with backspin) that moves more slowly and buys time for the teammate making a run.

Accuracy

- Players should know how to serve both short and long passes to their targeted teammate or to the space the teammate is preparing to occupy.
- Although soccer players also pass with their heads, chests, and thighs, they should use their feet whenever possible if passing for accuracy is the objective.

Teams with great passing abilities can move the ball efficiently and attack quickly, giving the defense less time to recover and get organized behind the ball. Teams that have learned to serve various types of passes are successful at getting players in the box for that final pass in the attacking third, putting players in dangerous positions for scoring opportunities.

Although the emphasis in this chapter is on the technical and tactical elements necessary for good passing in the field, it is important to remember that the ability to pass the ball is also valuable for goalkeepers. Goalkeepers need to spend time on their passing techniques so that their teammates feel confident passing a ball back to them when they run out of passing options, or are trying to switch the field. Goalkeepers that develop good passing and kicking techniques can and should take their own goal kicks, which frees up a defensive player in those set play situations.

Types of Passes

Passing can be broken down essentially into short-range and long-range passes, which vary in distance depending on the age and technical ability of the player.

Short-Range Passes

For most high school athletes, passes that are less than 30 yards are considered short-range passes. Short-range passes are used to maintain possession and are typically passed on the ground so the receiving player can control the ball easily. Because it is easier to hit a target that is closer to you, most teams try to maintain possession of the ball with short-range passes. The three types of short-range passes are the inside of the foot pass, the outside of the foot pass, and chipping.

Inside of the foot pass   The inside of the foot pass is typically used when a player needs to send a ball with good speed to move the ball quickly up the field. The inside of the foot pass is most common for short-range passing because it is the most accurate; the large surface area of the foot allows for good contact with the ball.

When preparing to execute an inside of the foot pass, the athlete should be square to the passing direction or target, meaning that the head, shoulders, trunk, and hips are turned toward the direction of the pass (see figure 9.1a). The player's plant foot is placed next to the ball with the toe pointing in the direction the player wants the ball to travel. The kicking foot should be positioned sideways so the inside of the foot is open toward the ball and the toe faces out and up. The arms are kept up and out for balance, and the head is over the ball. To execute the pass, the player locks the ankle and swings the

Figure 9.1   The inside of the foot pass requires the kicking foot to swing through the ball with the toe up and the ankle locked.

kicking leg through the center of the ball with the inside surface of the foot (see figure 9.1*b*) and performs a short follow-through toward the target.

Outside of the foot pass The outside of the foot pass is used for short- and medium-range passes when a player needs to send a pass while dribbling at speed. This type of pass is excellent for deception because the player doesn't give away the direction of the pass with the hips and plant foot, and it lets her continue her movement forward without any change in stride. The outside of the foot pass is not as accurate as the inside of the foot pass because the athlete is moving with speed. The pass is deceptive and unpredictable because the athlete does not square up her hips to face the target. When done correctly, the outside of the foot pass can create a spin on the ball, making it difficult for the opponent to read.

When preparing to execute an outside of the foot pass, the player faces the direction of the attack and places the plant foot slightly behind and to the side of the ball (see figure 9.2*a*). The arms are out for balance, and the head is down and steady. When executing the pass, the athlete must use an inside-out kicking motion. She makes contact with the inside of the ball using the outside surface of the instep (see figure 9.2*b*). The player

should not draw back from the hip with a full swing, but rather snap the leg forward from the knee down to create a pass with pace. The follow-through should be directly toward the target.

Chipping Chipping is generally considered an advanced short pass, but more skilled players can execute it as a long-range pass. Chipping is generally used to get the ball to a teammate over an opponent who is in the way of the passing lane. It can also be used as a shot on goal when the goalkeeper is off her line. The chip can be used during regular play or during a free kick to try to get the ball behind a wall of defenders and into the running path of a teammate.

When preparing to chip the ball, the athlete should approach the ball from a slight angle and place the plant foot slightly behind the ball (see figure 9.3*a*). To execute the pass, the player draws the kicking leg back, keeping the toe down and the foot extended (see figure 9.3*b*). The player's hips and shoulders should be square with the target as the foot makes contact with the ball as low as possible, using a short, lower-leg chop, or kicking motion, with very little follow-through. Chopping underneath the ball will give it some backspin, making it easier for the receiving teammate to control the pass.

Figure 9.2 When executing the outside of the foot pass, the athlete uses an inside-out kicking motion with the outside surface of the instep.

Figure 9.3 To chip the ball, the athlete uses a short lower-leg snap to create backspin and very little follow-through.

Long-Range Passes

Long-range passes are used for passing the ball to a teammate or into the space a teammate is moving to occupy when the distance between the player with the ball and the target is at least 30 yards. Long-range passing is used to cover more distance in a shorter amount of time and enables a team to get into its attacking third in the hope of setting up scoring opportunities. Long-range passing is important for speed of play because the ball arrives to its target sooner, or it catches the opposing players off balance on a quick counterattack, giving them less time to recover or get behind the ball. Long-range passing also allows players to get in behind the defense and force them to retreat as they track runs or chase down the ball. It is an excellent way to switch the field and force the opponent to shift toward the ball and spread out, creating more passing channels for your team. The three primary long-range passes are the driven instep pass, the flighted instep pass, and the bent pass.

Driven instep pass The most powerful of the long-range passes is performed by using the instep (or laces) of the foot to move the ball. The instep gives the athlete a fairly flat, hard surface to strike the ball with. Passes can be on the ground or in the air and cover a great distance, allowing a team to play fast and attack quickly. This pass is difficult to perform accurately because the distance of the target and pressure from opponents can cause players to neglect squaring up their shoulders and hips and fail to produce a complete follow-through. However, a team that has mastered this skill increases its speed of play because of the distance and pace at which the ball travels.

When preparing to pass with the instep, the player should place the plant foot next to or just slightly in front of the ball, with the knee bent over the ball (see figure 9.4a). The shoulders and hips are square to the target, the arms are out for balance, and the head is down. To execute the pass, the player brings the kicking leg back with the toe pointed down and the foot extended (see figure 9.4b). The player makes contact with the center of the ball (see figure 9.4c). Note that if the athlete is trying to send the ball higher, she should strike it lower. During the kicking motion, the lower leg snaps, becoming the source of power. The swing of the leg from the hip helps with the follow-through and accuracy of the pass. The follow-through should be straight toward the target, and the athlete should push off the plant foot during this phase (see figure 9.4d).

Figure 9.4 The driven instep pass requires the athlete to keep the toe down and the ankle locked in order to snap from the lower leg and follow through toward the target.

Flighted instep pass A flighted instep pass is a long-range passing technique used when a player needs to serve a ball over a long distance. It has a higher flight path so it can go over opponents' heads. Because of the flight pattern of this pass, it is also used when a pass needs to be delayed for a teammate making a run.

When preparing to execute a flighted instep pass, the plant foot is slightly behind the ball, while the toe is pointed in the direction of the pass (see figure 9.5a). The ankle of the kicking foot is locked, and the toe is turned slightly out. The arms are out for balance, the shoulders are square with the target, and the head is steady with the eyes on the ball. To execute the pass, the kicking leg swings toward the target. Contact is made below the middle portion of the ball with the center of the instep (see figure 9.5b). The kicking leg follow-through is toward the target

and upward to lift the ball as the player leans back slightly (see figure 9.5c). Again, the lower-leg snap helps create the pace of the pass. The lower the player makes contact on the ball, the higher the serve will be and the more backspin there will be on the ball. Backspin makes it easier for the teammate receiving the ball because the ball slows down once it hits the ground and therefore does not typically have to be chased.

Figure 9.5 The flighted instep pass requires the athlete to lock the ankle of the striking foot while making contact below the middle portion of the ball to achieve height and backspin.

Bent pass   A bent pass is a long-range pass that has a curved, or bent, flight pattern. It enables the athlete to send a ball around an opponent who is in the way of a direct pass to a teammate. Because playing a bent ball is an advanced skill, athletes must first learn to control how they contact and follow through on flighted and driven balls before attempting the bent ball. Once mastered, bent balls can be dangerous passes that can send the ball behind defenses. This passing technique can be valuable for keeping the ball in play when a player has run out of room near the sideline or end line.

When preparing to bend a ball, the athlete should approach the ball at an angle; in other words, the body does not face the target directly. As the athlete plants next to the ball, the knee is slightly bent, the arms are out for balance, and the head is down with the eyes on the ball (see figure 9.6a). To execute the pass, the player leans back slightly and contacts the ball slightly to the left or right of the center of the ball, striking across the ball rather than through the middle of the ball (see figure 9.6b). The athlete contacts the ball with a "slicing" motion with the inside (or outside) of the foot. The follow-through is curved following the path of the ball, which creates the curved flight pattern (see figure 9.6c).

Passing Activities

As mentioned previously, the components of passing—pace, timing, and accuracy—can all be learned and improved on as long as your athletes are willing to commit to practicing these skills on their own in addition to the team setting.

The following passing drills will teach your athletes when and how to execute the correct passing techniques for a variety of tactical situations while becoming more confident on the ball.

Cone Knockdown

Objectives   To develop accurate passes, improve speed of play, and learn to pass accurately with a variety of surfaces.

Description   Divide players into groups of six to eight; each player has a partner. Set up a grid for each group, approximately 15 × 25 yards. At each end of the grid, spread five cones along the end line (see figure 9.7). Position a group of two for each team (X and O) inside the grid and designate which direction they are attacking. They must attempt to knock down their cones

Figure 9.6   To bend a pass, the athlete contacts the ball in a slicing motion with the inside or outside of the foot.

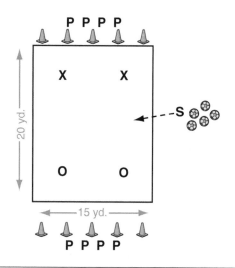

Figure 9.7 Cone Knockdown.

with various types of passes (inside of the foot, outside of the foot, and instep). If a ball goes out of bounds at the sideline of the grid or a team scores by knocking down a cone, the server (S) plays in a new ball. If a shot is taken and misses the cones, the opposing team brings the ball back in play with a pass from the end line. Teams battle each other for two minutes trying to knock their own cones down while keeping the opposing team from scoring. The team with the most cones down at the end of two minutes, or the team that knocks all its cones down before time is up, is the designated winner. Organize a championship round with the top teams from each grid. Teams waiting to play (P) should spread out along the end lines to collect balls.

Three-Grid Transition

Objectives To develop passing accuracy and improve receiving, angles of support, and combination play.

Description Create three teams of four or five players each, and give each team a different color. Younger or less experienced teams should play with three or four players to keep the drill simple. Create a large grid, approximately 70 × 40 yards, and divide it into three sections. Create two end zones that are 30 × 40 yards with cones on each end and a 10-yard neutral zone in the middle of the two areas. Place a team in each of the three zones. The remaining teams (P) are near the server juggling and doing sit-

ups and push-ups while waiting for their turns (see figure 9.8).

The server (S) begins play by serving a ball to a team in one of the end zones (X). Players must get five successful passes before they can pass the ball through the neutral zone to the opposite end zone. Successful passes on the ground are worth 2 points; balls in the air are worth 1 point. The team in the neutral zone (N) tries to prevent the team with the ball from successfully sending a pass by having two players go into the end zone and play defense, while the other two or three players remain in the neutral zone and deny a through pass.

If the team in possession is successful in passing to the opposite zone, the neutral team must now transition into the new grid to prevent the team in the other end zone (O) from scoring. Any two players from the neutral zone can transition as long as only two go into the end zone while the others remain in the neutral zone. If the defensive team is successful in winning the ball or denying the pass, that ball becomes dead and the defensive team now takes over the end zone and waits for the opposing team to send them a pass.

Play continues by the server serving a new ball to the opposite end zone. Now the team that lost possession becomes the new neutral team and must transition to the neutral zone while two of its players run into the possession team's zone to deny a pass. Play continues in this fashion with teams constantly transitioning from end zones to neutral zones based on successful passes and loss of possession. Rotate waiting teams in every five minutes.

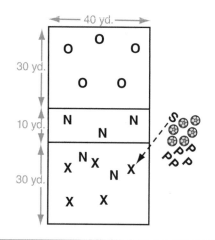

Figure 9.8 Three-Grid Transition.

Variations

- Play with fewer players, create smaller grids, or limit the number of touches or types of passes.
- Have the resting team become the new defending team having to win the ball and successfully pass to the opposite zone to remain in the new zone.

Sequential Passing

Objectives To develop direct and accurate passing and an awareness and understanding of the importance of movement off the ball, and to anticipate passing angles.

Description Divide players into groups of six to eight and give each athlete a number. You can use the penalty box or make smaller grids with cones. Players must pass the ball sequentially, receiving the ball from the number before them and passing the ball to the number after them. Players must be moving at all times and can make passes from any distance within the grid. Play should start with a pass from player 1 to player 2 and through to player 8; players should then work their way back down from player 8 to player 1.

Variations

- Every other player takes a turn as a defender and tries to keep the group from making successful sequential passes. For example, if player 3 is in the middle, then player 2 would pass to player 4, and so on.
- Limit players to passes of only one or two touches.
- Add a second ball and encourage speed of play.

Center Circle

Objectives To develop accurate passing and improve receiving under pressure, speed of play, and the ability to pass and exchange positions within a defined area quickly and efficiently.

Description Divide players into an offensive and defensive team and have them play in the center circle in the middle of the field, or use cones to create a circle of the same size. The offensive team spreads six players around the circle and has one player in the middle (this player should rotate with the outer players; players take responsibility for rotating in). The defensive team is outside the circle and next to the server. Play begins by the server (or coach) playing a ball to any circle player. When a ball is played, the defensive team sends three players into the circle to prevent the offensive team from getting five consecutive passes.

Five consecutive passes equals 1 point. When a ball goes out of bounds or gets interrupted by the defenders, the server plays a new ball, and three new defenders must transition in to prevent the passes. Emphasize speed of play. The defensive team must be organized and ready to send three new players on every transition of a new ball. Give teams two to three minutes to score as many points as possible and then rotate them from offense to defense and vice versa. Give teams two or three rounds to accumulate points. Players should verbally call out points each time they score.

Variations

- Limit the number of touches offensive players can make.
- Change the number of defenders that can enter the circle.
- Make the grid smaller or larger depending on the age and technical level of your team.

RECEIVING

Receiving the ball—also referred to as trapping the ball—is viewed as more of an active skill in today's game and is referred to as a player's first touch. Many athletes think that receiving a ball is just a matter of collecting the ball and keeping it close to the body. When I was young, our trapping practice consisted of pulling the ball in and keeping it close, taking a second touch to set it up, and then sending it with a third touch. In truth, proper receiving requires the player, on her first touch, to take pace off the ball, anticipate where the ball should go, and use the proper surface to receive the ball and execute the next move. Let's look at these a little more closely:

Taking Pace Off the Ball

- Remain low, balanced, and centered over the plant leg.

- Cushion the ball by withdrawing a little as the ball hits the surface.

- Control the pace while redirecting it in the desired direction.

Anticipating Where the Ball Should Go

- Get in the proper position and line the body up behind the ball to receive it properly.

- Use the first touch to prepare for the next move based on what is happening on the field.

- Play the first touch with the purpose of passing long to a teammate to take or create space, take on an opponent, or take a shot on goal.

Knowing Which Surface of the Foot to Use

- Use the proper surface based on the flight trajectory of the ball and whether there is pressure from an opponent.

- Use the largest surface of the foot when possible.

- Keep your eye on the ball.

Types of Receives

An athlete can receive the ball several ways depending on whether it was passed on the ground or in the air. Ground balls can be received with the inside of the foot, the outside of the foot, the instep, or the sole of the foot. Balls are received out of the air using the instep, thigh, chest, or head.

When teaching your players how to properly receive a ball, emphasize the importance of control first. Explain that the first touch is really a preparation touch for the next move. Once your athletes become skilled in the mechanics of receiving, they will be able to combine control of the ball with quick, tactical decision making.

Receiving Balls on the Ground

When receiving balls on the ground, a player can use any of the main surfaces typically used to pass the ball; that is, the instep, the inside of the foot, or the outside of the foot. The surface used depends on where the ball is coming from, whether there is pressure from an opponent, and what the player wants to do with it next.

Receiving with the instep A player will typically receive the ball with the instep when she has the time and space to take a bigger touch and penetrate forward. Receiving the ball with the instep allows the athlete to continue running without breaking stride, allowing her to cover more ground while pushing the ball farther in front without losing possession. This type of receiving is one of the most difficult in soccer, but it is very efficient. Receiving with the instep is useful when trying to control a long ball that is dropping at a steep angle, or when trying to bring a loose ball in the air down to the ground.

When receiving with the instep, the player must follow the flight of the ball and move her body to position herself to get directly behind it. As she moves into position to bring the ball down with the upper part of the foot, both the receiving and the plant leg should be bent at the knee. Contact should be made with the instep parallel to the ground. The moment the ball makes contact with the foot, the athlete pulls the receiving leg slightly backward while catching the ball on the top of the flexed foot to help absorb the force of the pass (see figure 9.9).

Figure 9.9 Receiving a ball on the ground with the instep.

Using this surface allows the player to continue her running motion when receiving the ball.

Receiving with the inside of the foot A player will typically receive the ball with the inside of the foot when she is facing the attacking direction and has the time and space to open up the hips and receive the ball across her body with her downfield foot. Ideally, when receiving with the inside of the foot, the player also has the opportunity to take a look prior to receiving the ball and has already decided where her next touch will send the ball and whether she has time to dribble and attack the space, pass to a teammate, or take a shot on goal.

When receiving the ball with the inside of the foot, the athlete's plant leg is slightly bent so that she can move the ball while taking an active touch away from the pressuring opponent. The hips are open allowing the foot to be perpendicular to the body, and the ankle is flexed (locked) with the toe up, providing a large surface area for contact with the ball (see figure 9.10). Contact with the ball should be made just slightly above the middle of the ball to keep it low, particularly when receiving a bouncing ball. The athlete should move toward the ball to receive it as early as possible, and the arms should be extended out to the side to help maintain balance, while the head is down only

briefly to collect the ball. The player should use the center of the inside of the foot to cushion the ball and absorb the ball's momentum. The athlete's body should be relaxed and the plant foot light to prepare for her next move. Being successful with this type of receiving is important for soccer players because it is routinely used in game situations to settle balls received on or near the ground.

Receiving with the outside of the foot. A player will typically receive the ball with the outside of the foot when she is under pressure or when her back is to the attacking goal. Receiving a ball with the outside of the foot is best when moving away from a defender in a lateral (left or right) direction so that the player can create her next move by gaining more space between the ball and the opponent. In addition, when receiving with the outside of the foot, a player should work to position sideways to her opponent so that she can get her body between the pressuring defender and the ball. Although keeping the back to the defender can work, good defenders can still reach in and poke a ball away because there is not much space between them and the ball. With the player's body sideways to the defender and the ball on the outside of the foot, the defender will have difficulty reaching the ball without causing a foul.

Figure 9.10 Receiving a ball on the ground with the inside of the foot.

Figure 9.11 Receiving a ball on the ground with the outside of the foot.

When receiving the ball with the outside of the foot, the athlete should position her body sideways between the opponent and the ball as the ball arrives. Using the foot farthest from the opponent, the athlete should rotate the receiving foot inward, toe down, and receive the ball on the outside surface of the instep (see figure 9.11). Depending on the pace of the ball, the athlete should cushion the pass by withdrawing the receiving leg slightly as the ball hits the foot. The knees should remain flexed and the body low while pushing the ball in the direction of the next move.

Receiving with the sole of the foot New and younger players are often taught to receive with the sole of the foot because they can use the ground to help them stop the ball. This style of receiving is typically used for a ball that will bounce just before reaching the player. However, if the ball is passed with a lot of pace, it can be difficult to stop and often ends up going under the player's foot. Therefore, usually only advanced players are comfortable using the sole of the foot for receiving balls. Some players like to use this technique because the ball stays in front of them, allowing them to keep their heads up and make quick decisions about their next moves. Those who become efficient at receiving with the sole of their foot can receive and escape pressure in one movement.

When receiving the ball with the sole of the foot, the athlete must get in line with the incoming pass by moving her feet, allowing her to receive the ball in a balanced and low stance. She should remain light on her feet while keeping her arms out for balance. As the ball hits the ground, the athlete puts the sole of the foot on the ball, redirecting it back to the ground (see figure 9.12). The arms are extended for balance as the body leans back slightly with the receiving foot locked and extended toward the ball. The plant leg remains light with the knee slightly bent, which aids in cushioning the ball because it allows the body to give or soften on contact. Contact with the ball is made in front of the body, and the toe of the receiving foot is up so contact with the ball is made with the middle of the sole.

Receiving Balls in the Air

An active first touch is much more difficult when receiving balls in the air than when receiving

Figure 9.12 Receiving a ball on the ground with the sole of the foot.

balls on the ground. The player must make a decision about the proper surface with which to bring the ball down to the ground and set it up in order to play it quickly and efficiently with the next touch—all based on the service (pass) and flight of the ball. Essentially four surfaces can be used when receiving the ball in the air: the instep, the thigh, the chest, and the head (for more information on heading, see chapter 11).

Receiving with the instep Receiving with the instep is typically the easiest way to bring the ball out of the air and directly to the ground, unless of course the ball is too high and the athlete does not have time to let the ball drop because of pressure from the opponent. Athletes should learn to use the instep when they are not under immediate pressure and have time to let the ball drop to knee height or lower. With practice, using this surface prepares the player quickly for the next touch because the ball is on the ground with one touch, unlike the thigh and chest traps that usually require a second touch before the ball is ready to be played.

When receiving with the instep, the athlete must first anticipate the flight of the ball while moving to get directly behind it. To contact the ball, the athlete's body should be low and balanced and the arms should be out wide for balance. The plant leg is bent at the knee, and the

Figure 9.13 The athlete follows the path of the ball and aligns the foot when receiving a ball in the air with the instep.

receiving foot is raised off the ground with the knee bent and the toe pointed so that the foot is parallel to the ground (see figure 9.13*a*). The receiving foot is kept firm as the player makes contact, and the toe slightly flexes as she moves her leg and foot down with the path of the ball, bringing it to the ground (see figure 9.13*b*).

Receiving with the thigh Receiving a ball in the air with the thigh is used when the ball is dropping too high to use the instep, but is still below the chest. This type of receive is best used when defensive pressure is coming from behind and the athlete can position her body between the opponent and the ball. The thigh is not the best choice to receive a ball if pressure is coming from the front because there is not enough time to let the ball drop to the thigh before the opponent has an opportunity to get to it.

When receiving with the thigh, the athlete's body should be low and balanced and the arms should be out wide for balance. To contact the ball, the player bends the plant leg at the knee and raises the thigh of the receiving leg until it is parallel to the ground while lifting the foot and placing it slightly behind the body (see figure 9.14). The thigh moves toward the ball and downward on contact to cushion and take pace off the ball. This movement stops the forward momentum of the ball and helps it drop to the ground in front of the

body. If the thigh is moving toward the ball at the moment of contact, the ball will bounce off the thigh and be difficult to control.

Figure 9.14 While slightly bending the plant leg, the athlete lifts the receiving thigh up so that it is parallel to the ground while cushioning the ball down toward the ground.

Receiving with the chest Receiving a ball in the air with the chest can be used when an athlete is receiving a high ball and pressure is coming from behind. The athlete can put her body between the opponent and the oncoming ball and use the chest to receive it. Receiving with the chest should not be used if the athlete is under immediate pressure from the front because the ball is exposed from the time it hits the chest until it comes down to the foot. If frontal pressure is there, the athlete may not have time to take a second touch before the opponent arrives.

When receiving with the chest, the athlete's upper body should be relaxed, and there should be a slight bend at the waist and knees. The ath-lete's back is arched to take some of the pace off the ball, and the arms are out wide for balance and to help withdraw the upper body as the ball arrives to cushion the impact. If the pass is low, the athlete can position the chest downward to direct the ball toward the ground (see figure 9.15, *a* and *b*). If the pass is high or driven, the chest must be angled upward to create a flatter surface, allowing the ball to drop from the chest and then be played out of the air with a second touch (see figure 9.16, *a* and *b*). Players with advanced skills can redirect the ball with one touch by moving or turning the chest to the left or right and deflecting the ball to the side of a defender, allowing the athlete to pass or shoot the ball out of the air and off a volley.

Figure 9.15 When the ball is served low, the athlete bends at the waist and knees while receiving the ball in the air with the chest.

Figure 9.16 When receiving the ball out of the air with the chest, the athlete bends at the waist and knees while cushioning the ball and creating a flat surface.

Receiving Activities

When learning to receive balls, both on the ground and in the air, athletes can improve their first touch significantly with practice. Be creative and change drills to fit the needs of your team. Make receiving drills fun and competitive by changing the rules and setting goals for your players to meet (note that any of the drills used in passing can be used for receiving as well). Also, remind your athletes of the importance of making the time to train on their own, particularly if they are struggling to find success in the drills at practice.

The following receiving drills will teach your athletes when and how to execute the correct receiving techniques for a variety of tactical situations while becoming more confident on the ball.

Receiving Circle

Objectives To develop receiving with various surfaces without defensive pressure and to improve passing accuracy.

Description Divide the team into two groups. One group forms a circle approximately the size of the center circle; each player forming the circle has a ball. The second group spreads out within the circle. Players on the inside of the circle check to a player on the outside, who passes the ball to the checking player. On your instruction, have players receive the ball with various surfaces. Start with balls played on the ground; then progress to knee, thigh, chest, and head height. Players receiving the ball must receive, then play the ball back to the passer, or receive, turn, and pass to a new player on the outside of the circle. Players must practice receiving with the inside of the foot, the outside of the foot, and the instep; take a lateral touch; and pass back with accuracy.

Variations

- Have players look over their shoulders as they check to the ball to get in the habit of looking for the opponent and making decisions about turning and passing.
- Divide players into three groups and have the third group in the middle act as defenders, providing pressure when receiving.

Snap Passing and Receiving

Objectives To develop receiving with the inside and outside of the foot and quickly move the ball laterally, before accurately passing the ball.

Description Players are divided into pairs. Make as many grids as you have partners. Grids consist of two cones one yard apart and another set of two cones 10 to 15 yards away. One player (P1) is positioned next to one cone on one end, and the other player (P2) is positioned opposite this player, next to a cone on the other end (see figure 9.17). P1 starts by passing the ball with her right foot to the cone where P2 is positioned. When P2 receives the ball, she must use the inside or outside of the foot to move the ball laterally to the cone one yard away with as few touches as possible, keeping the ball close. When she reaches that cone, she passes the ball back to P1, who is now waiting by the cone opposite her. Partners complete as many full cycles as possible in a 60-second time frame. A cycle, which equals 1 point, is when the ball gets back to P1. Players rotate after 60 seconds and pass with the left foot in a clockwise formation. Players keep track of their points and must call out their scores each time they add a point.

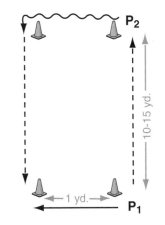

Figure 9.17 Snap Passing and Receiving.

TURNING

Turning with the ball is used in conjunction with receiving and is often an overlooked skill. Proper turning requires the athlete to receive the ball, turn with it, and penetrate forward with the goal of facing the defender as quickly as possible with the ball under control.

When receiving the ball, many players turn their backs to pressure when they could easily spin out of pressure or turn and face their opponents. Athletes' decision-making processes can improve if they learn to "take looks" before, during, and after receiving the ball. Top-level players are always looking to assess the situation and make decisions based on what the game dictates. However, looking around to assess the field when receiving the ball does not come naturally to many athletes, which is why they need to practice the skill of turning. As players reach higher levels of play, they need to be able to make decisions with their backs to the goal, and there are many options for turning and taking players on in this situation.

Before we learn about the types of turns your athletes can use in specific situations, let's look at a few keys points about turning in general:

• *Change speed when checking to receive the ball.* Your athletes need to get in the habit of checking hard (moving quickly toward the ball) and then slowing down as they receive it. A quick check will give the athlete more space between herself and the opponent, which gives her more time to decide what to do with the ball. Slowing down to receive the ball helps the athlete control the pass. If she receives the ball at a fast pace, the ball may bounce too far off her body and out of reach. Changing her pace when receiving the ball can also help her deceive the opponent, eliminating the opponent's ability to anticipate her next move.

• *Be completely confident with at least two turns.* Every athlete should have at least two "go-to" moves that she has perfected and knows she can perform if the situation lends itself to those moves. Mastering specific moves gives the athlete confidence in her abilities, motivates her to work hard, and adds more moves to her repertoire of skills. In addition, most moves are done in split-second situations in which the athlete does not have time to think about what move she should use. The athlete can rely on muscle memory if she has continually practiced and perfected a few specific moves.

• *Face up when possible.* When an athlete receives the ball with her back to the goal or an opponent, her options are limited. Teaching your athletes how to "face up," or turn with the ball to face the opponent, allows them to see their options and make quick decisions about whether to

dribble, pass, or shoot. When athletes learn how to receive and turn the ball against pressure, in tight space, they create more attacking options and are invaluable to the team.

• *Look to assess the situation and know where the defender is.* Emphasize to your players how to look around and over their shoulders when receiving balls with their backs to opponents. Taking a look prior to receiving the ball helps them decide what to do with the ball before it arrives. Looking over the shoulder lets them know which side the pressure is coming from and can help them turn away from that pressure or the incoming defender.

Types of Turns

As mentioned earlier, athletes must learn how take a look and make decisions based on the game situation. There are several ways to turn with the ball depending on the situation and what the player wants to do with the ball.

Outside of the Foot

Players can use the outside of the foot to turn away from, or spin off, the defender. This body position allows the athlete to lean into the defensive pressure and is used when the defender is marking tight. When an athlete wants to turn with the outside of the foot, she must first receive the ball with the foot farthest from the defender. The player can also position her body sideways so that she is between the defender and the ball, making it difficult for the defender to get to the ball. This position also allows her to see the defender and the available penetrating options and forces the defender to play on one shoulder to see or steal the ball.

When turning with the outside of the foot, the athlete leans into the defensive player by bending at the knees and getting her center of gravity low while keeping her arms out wide for balance. As the athlete leans into the defensive pressure, she can feint with her hips to one side and receive the ball with the opposite foot (see figure 9.18a). When contacting the ball, the athlete keeps the toe down and makes contact with the ball with the outside of the instep while spinning off the defender. This allows the ball to come off the foot to the side of the defender as the athlete follows the ball, puts the defender behind her, and moves the play forward (see figure 9.18b).

Figure 9.18   Turning by using the outside of the foot and spinning off the defender.

Facing Up

A player faces up when she has enough space and time to open up and turn toward the opponent. This movement requires that she continue checking to the ball, opening up and allowing the ball to come across the body while preparing it with the inside of the foot closest to the defender.

When facing up, the player must stop the momentum of the ball (see figure 9.19a) and turn in one continuous motion and keep the ball close so the first touch doesn't move it to the defender (see figure 9.19b).

Also, if the defender is closing in slowly on a player who is facing up, her first touch can be a little bigger and into the space between them. The receiving player can use the defender's momentum as she steps toward the defender in an effort to accelerate past her into a better attacking situation or to find a teammate to serve. If the defender is coming in fast and reckless, as they sometimes do, the athlete can use the defender's momentum against her by quickly pushing the ball laterally into space and stepping around the defender.

Figure 9.19   Facing up requires the athlete to turn in one continuous motion while keeping the ball close.

Cutting

A cut is when an attacking player creates space between herself and the defender by taking the defender away from the ball and then checking to the ball at an angle.

When cutting, with the defender at her back, the athlete takes a look over her shoulder to see where the defender is. When the defender is tight on the outside shoulder and moving fast, upon receiving the ball, the player takes a quick touch with the foot farthest from the defender (see figure 9.20a) and cuts (turns) the ball in the opposite direction (see figure 9.20b). The touch should be opposite the momentum of the defender, and the player must accelerate quickly before the defender can recover.

Spin Turn

A player uses a spin turn when she needs to change direction without exposing the ball to an opponent. There are numerous types of spin turns to use depending on the situation and where the player is on the field. For simplicity, we will discuss two of these turns.

One spin turn used by attacking players when pressure is coming from the front or the side that the pass was received from allows the player to penetrate the open space on the opposite side. This type of spin turn requires the player to step on top of the ball and pull it away with the sole of the foot, temporarily putting her body between the ball and the defender. For example, if the athlete collects the ball with the right foot, she places the sole of the right foot on the ball while spinning away from the opponent (see figure 9.21a). As she pulls the ball with the sole of her right foot, she uses her momentum and the pace of the pass and makes a 180-degree turn (spin), putting her body between the ball and the opponent (see figure 9.21b). She then moves the ball in the opposite direction using her left foot to push the ball forward and accelerate past the defender (see figure 9.21c).

Another type of spin turn is used by attacking players who are receiving the ball and cannot immediately go forward because of oncoming pressure from the front. The player steps past the ball with one foot and then turns it, moving it back in the direction of the pass with the outside of the same foot while "spinning out" of pressure. For example, as the athlete steps past the ball with her right foot, she temporarily puts her body between the ball and the oncoming opponent as she spins out (see figure 9.22a) and redirects the ball with the outside of her right foot (see figure 9.22b).

Figure 9.20 When the athlete cuts with the ball, the touch should be opposite the momentum of the defender.

Figure 9.21   When pressure is coming from the front or the side, the athlete pulls the ball with the sole of the foot while performing the spin turn.

Figure 9.22   Performing the spin turn when pressure does not allow a move forward requires the athlete to step past the ball and use the outside of the foot to spin out of pressure and back toward the direction of the pass.

Turning Activities

Turning with the ball is just one of the many choices an athlete has when receiving the ball. Players must practice to become efficient at this skill. As they improve and play at higher levels, playing with their backs to the goal happens more frequently because the game is faster and opponents are quicker to apply pressure. Players will have less time and space to make decisions and must learn how to turn, or spin, out of pressure. Improving their ability to receive a ball in intense situations and knowing what to do with it gives athletes the confidence they will need during the course of a game.

The following turning drills will teach your athletes when and how to execute the correct turning techniques for a variety of tactical situations while becoming more confident on the ball.

Turn and Face Up

Objectives   To develop receiving and turning with defensive pressure and accurate passing, as well as communication and fitness.

Description   Divide players into groups of four; each group has a grid of approximately 10 × 15 yards, with two small goals (1 to 2 yards wide) on each end line. Two players from each group (X and O) stand behind the end lines on each side and act as servers while they wait their turn. The other two players from the groups play 1v1 in the grid (see figure 9.23). Play begins with a ball passed from one server to a receiving player (O), who tries to turn on the defender (X) and go to the opposite goal. If the defender wins the ball, she must pass it to the player on her end line before turning and shooting on goal. If a ball goes out of bounds, the server (or first person in line) of the player who gets possession plays a new ball to the player as play continues. Rotate players every two minutes.

Variations

- Allow the server to enter play, creating a 2v1 situation.

- Instead of using small goals, players can score by passing to the player on the opposite end line for a point. The player on the end line can move back and forth to make herself available for the pass.

- Allow a limited or an unlimited number of passes back to the end line player to keep play moving.

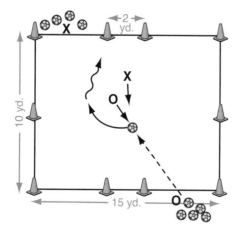

Figure 9.23   Turn and Face Up.

Pressure Receiving and Turning

Objective   To develop confidence in receiving and turning with full defensive pressure and speed of play.

Description   Divide players into groups of three. Each group has one-mini goal (2 yards wide) and a few balls. Two players, one defensive and the other offensive, line up by the goal; the server stands 15 yards away with balls. The offensive player checks to the server, and the defender follows with full pressure. The offensive player must receive the ball, turn on the defender, and try to beat her by dribbling through the cones for a point. All three players rotate every two or three turns. Players keep track of points. Have players practice the turns described in the Turning section of this chapter. Emphasize taking a look over their shoulders to help make the best tactical decision based on the defensive pressure. Servers can give verbal cues to help offensive players. Insist on speed of play and quick transitions while players rotate positions.

Variations

- Use your standard goals and incorporate a goalkeeper.

- Give players the option of passing back to the server and creating a 2v1 situation.

- Set up two or three mini-goals, forcing players to decide which goal to target (dribble through) and allow a specific amount of time in which to score (e.g., 10 to 15 seconds).

CHAPTER 10 SHOOTING AND FINISHING

Although we've all heard the expression "Defense wins championships," your team must score to win. Scoring is the objective of every attack, and yet it is the most difficult task in soccer. Shooting is the technical process of striking the ball with power while using the instep. Finishing is defined as the way a player strikes the ball toward the goal in a given situation. The great finishers make decisive choices when they shoot. They have the ability to use either foot with power and accuracy, they anticipate well, and they remain composed under pressure. Attacking players put up with a lot of physical contact from aggressive defenders who are desperate to keep them away from their goal.

As a coach, you must teach your players the technical aspects of shooting and finishing, in addition to teaching them how to prepare an organized attack while setting up as many finishing opportunities as possible. To do this, athletes must first master all the techniques discussed in the previous chapters—that is, controlling the ball, dribbling to take on opponents, beating opponents with passing combinations, and receiving the ball properly to set themselves up with immediate shooting opportunities. The truth is, the longer you can prevent a team from scoring, the more frustrated they become. Technical ability and confidence in shooting are key ingredients that allow a team to get into the opponent's penalty box, where great scoring opportunities exist.

TYPES OF SHOTS

When faced with scoring opportunities, players can use several types of shots based on the situation. These include the instep; the volley and side volley; and bent, or swerving, shots.

Instep

Shooting with the instep—or the laces—is a technique used with a stationary or moving ball. The skill is similar to that of passing with the instep, as discussed in chapter 9 on page 74, except that the follow-through is much greater. A player shoots with the instep when she wants to shoot with power and accuracy. A ball that is hit properly with the instep has either no spin or a slight backspin and travels straight and fast through the air.

When shooting with the instep, the player approaches the ball from behind and at a slight angle. With a small hop, she plants the supporting foot next to the ball while flexing at the knee (see figure 10.1a). The arms are held out for balance, the head is low, and the eyes are focused on the ball. The player draws the kicking leg back and extends the kicking foot, snapping the kicking leg straight, driving the instep through the center of the ball (see figure 10.1b), and continuing along the target line. A powerful strike should pull the support foot off the ground as the player's body continues forward in an exaggerated follow-through and lands on the kicking foot (see figure 10.1c).

Figure 10.1 To shoot with the instep, the athlete snaps the kicking leg while driving the instep through the center of the ball and follows through along the target line.

Volley

A volley is a type of shot that is taken out of the air and is used when a player does not have time to bring the ball out of the air and to the ground before striking it. When executed properly, the volley can be an extremely powerful shot for your players to use. The key to a successful volley is making good, clean contact with the instep of the foot. One of the major mistakes that players make when volleying is swinging too hard at the ball.

When shooting using the volley technique, the player moves to the spot where she thinks the ball will drop, faces the ball, and aligns her shoulders square to the ball. The kicking leg is drawn back behind the body with the foot extended, and the knee of the plant leg is slightly flexed (see figure 10.2a). The arms are out for balance, and the head should remain steady as the athlete watches the ball. As the ball is on its way down, the athlete squares the shoulders and hips to the target while positioning the knee of the kicking leg above the ball. The player uses a short swing with the kicking leg and snaps it straight, contacting the center of the ball with the instep while keeping the foot extended and pointing down at the moment of contact with the ball (see figure 10.2b). The follow-through for the volley is short because the player's momentum remains forward (see figure 10.2c).

Figure 10.2 When volleying, the athlete uses a short swing with the kicking leg while keeping the foot extended and pointing down during contact.

Side Volley

A side volley is a type of shot that is taken out of the air and off to the side of the body. It is used when an athlete must shoot a ball that bounces, a ball that drops to the side of the body, or a ball that needs to be redirected out of the air into the area of the goal. Striking the ball out of the air is difficult enough, but doing it from the side of the body requires great technique.

When performing a side volley, the athlete should adjust her feet early to get behind the ball, and she should get set before the strike. Her weight should be on the supporting leg, with the arms out for balance. As the athlete tracks the ball, she draws the kicking leg back with the knee bent, the thigh parallel to the ground, and the kneecap pointing toward the target (see figure 10.3a). The athlete pivots (by making a half turn) on the plant foot toward the target and, using the instep of the kicking foot, hits through the ball, contacting it above the centerline of the ball to help keep the shot low and driven (see figure 10.3b). The athlete must get full extension and snap through the ball with the lower leg to hit the ball cleanly. She follows through by rotating the body toward the target as she drops the opposite shoulder and slightly "falls away" from the shot (see figure 10.3c).

Figure 10.3 To perform the side volley, the athlete gets behind the ball and gets set before striking the ball.

STRATEGIES FOR FINISHING

In soccer, finishing is the act of putting the ball in the back of the opponent's net. Great finishers learn to make choices when they shoot. They learn how to vary their shots depending on the way the ball is served and whether it is rolling, bouncing, or coming out of the air. They also have the ability to take these shots with either foot. In addition, because athletes must execute the proper shot under the pressures of limited time, limited space, fatigue, and aggressive opponents, scoring goals is one of the most difficult tasks in soccer. In actuality, finishing is considered more of a tactical aspect of shooting than a skill in and of itself. Following are a few key principles players should keep in mind when taking a shot on goal:

What Surface Should I Use Based on the Game Situation?

- First, consider your own skill level based on the situation.
- If the type of serve dictates a volley, but you cannot volley, you should set the ball up for a better shot if time permits.
- Learn what specific finishing techniques support particular serves.
- Learn to trust your instincts. Make a decision quickly and go with it.

What Type of Pass Did I Receive?

- For a ball rolling on the ground, use the instep to shoot the ball.
- For a ball rolling on the ground when you are near or in the six-yard box, use the inside of the foot for accuracy if power is not an issue.
- For a ball that is bouncing, use the side volley.
- For a ball in the air and dropping quickly, use the full or half volley if you are in the penalty area and do not have time to settle it.
- For a ball that hangs in the air, use your head.

When Should I Shoot Versus Use a Pass?

- When you have an open goal, or a goal with just the goalkeeper
- When you have only one player to beat, unless your pass can result in a first-time shot from a better angle
- When you see the goalkeeper out of position or too far off her line
- When weather conditions are extreme and the goalkeeper has a hard time holding on to the ball
- When you are in or near the penalty box and your pass will result in an off-sides call

How Many Players Does My Team Commit to the Attack?

- The number of players committed to the attack will depend on the team or coaching philosophy and the team formation. Ideally, at least six players should be committed to the attack.
- A balanced attack is key. Committing too many players can leave gaps in your defense.
- Learn how your team builds an attack and know whether it is direct or possession oriented. If it is direct, fewer players will be involved in the attack.
- Learn how your opponent plays and if they are looking for a quick counterattack with direct play so that they can catch your team with too many players forward.

What Type of Box Organization Does My Team Use?

- Organize yourselves in the penalty box based on where the defenders are, where the ball is, and where the ball is going (for more information on these concepts, refer to chapter 13).
- When a shot is taken, you should have a player running to the near and far post and a player running toward the goalkeeper; this is known as "framing the goal."
- Find the gaps between defenders. Teammates should anticipate and prepare for a pass between defenders.

- Every player is responsible for organizing the box. Vocal players especially should take on this role.

- Keep it simple. Although certain positions have specific assignments, when time is a factor, the closest player to the far post should make the far post run.

- Box organization does not apply only to offense; the same principles should be applied to your defensive organization.

SHOOTING ACTIVITIES

Give your athletes shooting drills that emphasize various technical and tactical decisions that will teach them when to shoot and how to deal with defensive pressure effectively. Athletes need to learn how to stay calm in front of the net and avoid getting anxious, which often forces them to shoot in a hurry or take too long and miss their opportunity. Ideally, players should be able to take a look, control the ball, and shoot in one polished movement.

As is true for all technical skills in soccer, the more athletes are willing to supplement team practice by practicing alone with a ball and a wall or a shooting partner, the more they will improve their technical ability as well as their confidence. Because the shots a player gets in 15 minutes against a wall far outnumber those she gets in a team shooting drill, all players should be encouraged to find the time to do it. Athletes who take the time to work on their own and become technically sound not only perform better at practice but also provide the coaching staff with the opportunity to set up more challenging tactical situations because they are skilled enough to compete successfully in that environment.

Have your players start with stationary balls while focusing on power first. The more repetition they get in this area, the more the muscles used in shooting will be strengthened. As the muscles involved in shooting are developed and proper technique becomes habit, the athletes can rely on muscle memory, the process used by the neuromuscular system to memorize motor skills, resulting in a skill becoming automatic. Muscle memory helps when hitting balls from greater distances or from an off-balanced position while fatigued. All this results in a forward who becomes dangerous in the attacking third under any circumstance! Progression within your shooting drills is key in training proper technique. Once your athletes are striking the ball successfully with a stationary ball, you can progress to moving balls and eventually add defensive pressure within organized, gamelike drills that require them to make decisions under pressure in a variety of situations.

The following shooting drills will teach your athletes when and how to execute the correct shooting techniques for a variety of tactical situations while becoming more confident on the ball.

Inside Shooting and Finishing Crosses

Objectives To develop shots from the top of the penalty box, timing and accuracy with shots from a crossed ball, and making runs to frame the goal.

Description Divide players into three groups (P), with the exception of the goalkeepers (GK), who are in goal. Two groups line up at the top of the penalty arc where it meets the top of the penalty box. The third group starts near the right sideline, lined up evenly with the other groups. A server (S) stands at the middle top of the arc with balls (see figure 10.4). The first player in the line to the right of the server makes a run toward the goal (1 to 2 yards) and then quickly checks back to receive a ball from the server.

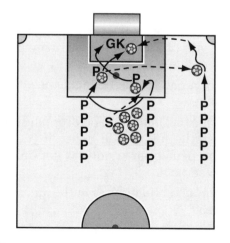

Figure 10.4 Inside Shooting and Finishing Crosses.

Upon receiving the ball, the player executes a one-touch pass to the first player in the line to the left of the server. This player can take a first-time shot on goal at the top of the penalty box; both players crash the goal to follow and finish any rebounds. If the second player does not have a good first-time shot, she passes to the first player in line on the flank. This player dribbles to the end line and sends a crossed ball into the 6-yard box. Both players from the inside lines make angled runs to frame the goal and finish the cross. Shooting players must collect their balls and return them to the server.

Play continues with the server sending a new ball after each shot. Players must transition quickly and rotate counterclockwise after each turn to play from each line. After approximately five minutes, the players on the flank move to the left sideline, and play continues as before, with the exception that the line to the left of the server now checks and receives balls first, in addition to the crosses coming from the left side. This drill is great for goalkeepers because they get a combination of shots and crosses and must be prepared for first-time shots.

Variations

- Add defensive players to make the drill more gamelike. You can add two flank lines and have the crosses come from either side.

- Add defenders and allow the attacking players to use the next person in each line to keep the ball in play.

- Award a corner kick to the offense if the ball goes off the goalkeeper or a defender.

Three-Tier Shooting

Objectives To develop three different shots on goal—a long shot, a passed shot, and a header—and to emphasize following shots to goal.

Description Divide players into three groups (P) and divide the balls equally among the groups. Group 1 lines up at the top of the penalty arc, group 2 lines up on the left side of the goalpost, and group 3 lines up on the right side of the goalpost (see figure 10.5). Play begins with the first player in group 1 taking a long shot

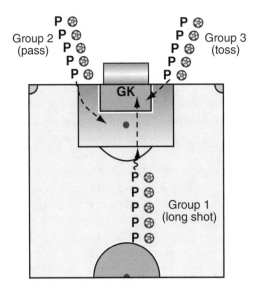

Figure 10.5 Three-Tier Shooting.

from the top of the arc. As she follows her shot, the first player in group 2 passes the ball to the middle of the penalty box for player 1 to take a shot while on the run toward the goal. Player 1 continues moving toward the goal and receives a toss from the first player in group 3. The toss should be at or near the top of the 6-yard box and target the head (players should always attempt to finish, regardless of the toss, and must volley if necessary). Players rotate clockwise once they've taken their turn. For example, after a player tosses from group 3, she then rotates to group 1, the player from group 1 goes to group 2, and so on. Goalkeepers rotate after every five or six shot rotations. Each player should go through the drill three to five times.

Variations

- Require specific types of shots with different surfaces.

- Add a trailing defender for pressure during shooting.

- Change one of the goalpost serves to a crossed ball or a finish off a volley.

Flying Changes

Objectives To develop an attacking and shooting mentality as well as decision making in the attack, combination play in front of the goal, and finishing techniques.

Description Divide players into two groups (X and O), each with a different color, and place each group next to the goal it will defend. Line up the players of each group at each post. The game is played in an area approximately 25 × 35 yards with two standard goals, one on each end line. A goalkeeper (GK) is in each goal. Balls are split equally between the teams and placed at the right post of each goal (see figure 10.6).

Play begins with the first player from each line competing in a 2v2 scrimmage. Players must look to shoot first, assist second, and possess third (this is an attacking game and so we are not as concerned about holding on to the ball). When a ball goes over the end line, the team whose end line it crossed must immediately get off the field and go to the end of their lines; two new players replace their teammates and come out with a new ball (balls always come from the right post). The other team's two players stay on to defend. In addition, when a goal is scored, two new players must replace the team that was scored on; the scoring team stays on to defend. If a ball goes out over the sideline, all four players are out and the team that would have had a throw-in brings in a new ball. Emphasize quick transitions from offense to defense.

After scoring, players must be mentally focused and prepared to defend two new shooters. This game must be played fast with many goal-scoring opportunities! This drill forces pressure situations in which players must have good first touches. Goalkeepers play the entire game unless you have a third goalkeeper who needs to rotate in.

Variations

- Add target players.
- Make the drill a 3v3 situation and add another line of flank players to incorporate more crossing.

Battle in the Box

Objectives To develop shooting and finishing techniques and to be the last one to touch the ball before it hits the back of the net.

Description Divide players into two groups (X and O). Separate each group into attackers and servers or shooters, and give each a different color. Half of each group gathers in the 6-yard box ready to battle, and the other half spreads out in an arc outside the penalty box. Each of these players has two balls and spreads out along the arc. Goalkeepers (GK) rotate in the goal (see figure 10.7).

The first player on the left side of the arc shoots on goal, and the players in the box try to direct the ball into the goal. The last player to touch the ball scores a point for her team. Note that the box gets very crowded, and the game becomes extremely physical as players try to get to the ball and finish it in the back of the net. As soon as the ball is in the back of the net or goes out of bounds, the next player on the arc shoots at goal and the battle continues.

If an arc player scores without the box players touching the ball, her team gets 2 points. Play

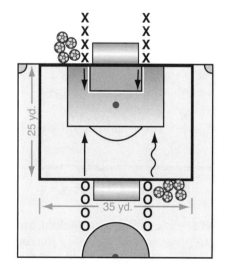

Figure 10.6 Flying Changes.

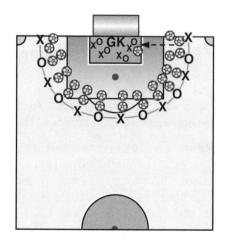

Figure 10.7 Battle in the Box.

continues with each arc player serving twice (shots start from one end of the arc and back again). Box and arc players rotate, so all players get a chance to shoot from the arc and battle in the box. Play two or three full rounds.

Variations

- Have the arc players serve only lofted balls or only low-driven balls.

- Play "anything goes." Literally, after the ball is served, play continues until a goal is scored no matter what it takes. Even if a ball goes over the end line, play continues! If it's in the bushes and players have to use their hands, play continues!

- Allow box players to pass back to the arc player if they cannot get a shot off to restart the drill.

CHAPTER 11 HEADING

Unique to the sport of soccer, the skill of heading is used to pass, shoot, and receive the ball. Some teams rely on heading the ball more than others do, depending on their style of play. Teams that play a lot of long balls rely on their forwards to win balls in the air. Regardless of your team's style, at this level there will always be heading opportunities during the course of the game.

Heading is used defensively to clear a long ball or cross out of the penalty box, and offensively to shoot toward the goal by getting on the end of a cross, corner kick, or free kick. It can also be used to pass to a teammate by flicking the ball with the head to change its flight pattern.

As the game has evolved, heading has become more important tactically. As a result, players have had to become better technically and to head more often in game situations. Of course, like any new skill, athletes must learn proper technique in progression. This is especially true for heading because there has been more dialogue recently about the long-term effects of frequent heading. If done incorrectly, heading can result in neck, head, or spinal injuries. As the number of concussions in soccer increases as a result of challenging balls in the air, more people are discussing requiring headgear in competitive environments. It is important to remember that the majority of concussions and head injuries happen from colliding with other players, not from heading the ball. Those collisions are typically a result of going up for a header, however, and therefore athletes should know the proper technique and how to protect themselves in the air.

When teaching heading to your players, keep these safety precautions in mind to reduce the risk of injury: (1) Emphasize proper technique, and (2) have your players practice heading frequently, but in short segments.

TYPES OF HEADING

There are two primary types of heading—defensive heading, which is typically used to clear a ball out of your defensive third by heading for height, distance, and width, and offensive (attacking) heading, which is used to pass or shoot on goal.

Defensive Heading

As mentioned, defensive heading is used for clearing the ball out of your defensive third of the field. Good defensive heading consists of these three qualities:

- *Height.* The ball should be cleared high to buy time for the defense to get organized.

• *Distance.* You want good distance to allow your team to get the ball away from the goal and out of your defensive end of the field.

• *Width.* Getting the ball wide and out to the flanks keeps it from landing in the middle of the field and at the foot of an attacking player who is ready to put it back on frame (or on the face of the goal).

Defenders typically have more success heading out the big, long balls played up the middle from their opponents' defense, or off a goal kick or free kick, than they do heading out crosses targeting forwards. These crosses are difficult to judge because they are usually driven and bending toward the goal. In this situation, the defender is usually running toward her own goal while marking a forward and must try to head the ball away from the goal. Inadvertently scoring for the opponent can happen in this situation because the defender is moving toward her goal but having to head the ball in the opposite direction. Defenders should concentrate on heading through the bottom half of the ball while heading it up and out as high and hard as possible. Your athletes need to develop the power and courage to attack the ball regardless of the challenge from the opposing forward.

Offensive Headers

As mentioned, offensive, or attacking, headers are used for passing or shooting on goal and are generally more difficult to perform than defensive headers. They are technically more demanding because they require the accuracy of hitting a target, which can either be a teammate (in the case of a pass) or the goal (in the case of a shot on goal), while focusing on hitting the ball with the proper surface, in the right spot, and with the right pace.

Offensive, or attacking, headers to goal generally require that the player direct the ball downward and away from the goalkeeper. The player's focus is on not only placement but also avoiding a moving target (a defensive player or goalkeeper). Because of the directional requirements of attacking headers, your athletes will benefit from training that requires receiving the ball from one direction and heading toward another.

HEADING TECHNIQUE

As we've already mentioned, learning proper heading technique is essential because heading is used in both attacking and defending situations. Your athletes should be prepared to use essentially three heading techniques in a game: the jump header, the diving header, and the flicked (or flick-on) header. However, before you teach these headers to your athletes, first teach them proper heading technique without a jump from a seated position, then a kneeling position, and finally a standing position using a stationary ball. This learning progression is important because many players have difficulty properly tracking the ball and timing their contact with it. If a player jumps too early, the ball hits the top of her head as she is coming down from the jump. The timing needs to be such that the athlete is heading through the center of the ball and attacking it, rather than being hit on the head by the ball. The best way to teach this is to first practice the skill of heading without a jump.

Seated Headers

Practicing proper heading technique in a seated position helps isolate the movement of the head and neck. Group players in pairs with one sitting on the ground with her knees bent and the other standing. The standing partner throws an underhand toss for the seated player. The seated player heads the ball back to her partner's hands.

The seated player pulls the head back and strikes the ball with the forehead at the hairline (see figure 11.1, *a* and *b*). The elbows are bent, and the hands and arms are parallel with the shoulders. As the player initially pulls the trunk back, the head and neck drive forward through the ball along the target line of the toss. The upper body moves slightly forward with this movement, but the hips and trunk are fairly stationary throughout the drill. The eyes should remain open and the mouth closed. The athlete should practice heading the ball higher by hitting it slightly below the centerline, as well as heading the ball down by striking it above the centerline.

Players should concentrate on the quality of the header. Partners rotate every 5 to10 headers. More advanced players can also incorporate sit-ups with this drill; the seated player starts on her back with her knees bent and

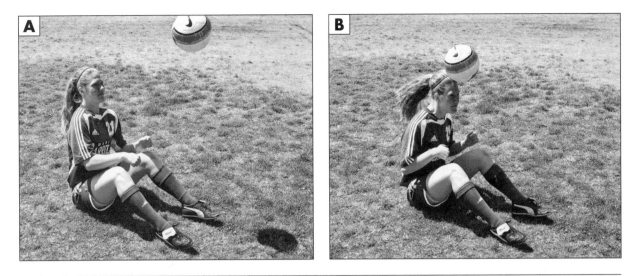

Figure 11.1   Heading the ball from a seated position helps isolate the movement of the head and neck.

curls up toward the toss, heading the ball with proper heading technique. After each header, the athlete lowers her back to the ground to complete the sit-up and prepare for the next toss. The tosser can vary the distance of the toss, forcing her partner to work on timing her contact with the ball.

Kneeling Headers

Once players have mastered seated heading, the next phase is heading from a kneeling position. This phase emphasizes the flexion and exten-sion of the trunk while combining the motion of the head and neck. Players are grouped in pairs with one player in a kneeling position with her hands resting initially near her lap. The standing partner tosses the ball, and the kneeling player bends the trunk back as the arms and hands become parallel with the shoulders, elbows bent (see figure 11.2*a*). The kneeling player drives the trunk forward as the head strikes through the ball, using proper heading technique (see figure 11.2*b*) and with enough momentum to cause the player to fall forward onto her hands (see figure 11.2*c*). The tosser should alternate

Figure 11.2   Heading the ball from a kneeling position emphasizes the flexion and extension of the trunk combined with the head and neck motion.

between high and low tosses, and partners should switch every 5 to10 headers.

Standing Headers

After players have mastered both seated and kneeling headers, they can progress to standing and heading stationary balls. Players are grouped in pairs of similar heights. One player stands with the ball held out in front of her body and overhead (see figure 11.3a). The other player stands underneath and slightly behind the ball and jumps straight up with a two-foot takeoff to make contact with the ball (see figure 11.3b). The jump should be explosive using the legs to send the body upward. The arms will open up, elbows bent, and assist the jump by driving them up and then down with the momentum of the jump. The player should make contact with the ball using proper heading technique and explode through the ball. If necessary, you can start the drill by having the athlete just make contact with the ball, then try to explode through the movement and head the ball out of her partner's hands.

Jump Headers

Once your players have mastered the technique of heading from a seated, kneeling, and standing position, the focus can shift to the game-related skill of jump headers. The previous drills are used only as a building block to teach and reinforce proper heading technique. The progression began with the emphasis on the movement of the head and neck, moved on to the flexion and extension of the trunk, and finished with a two-foot takeoff to head a ball directly overhead, held stationary in a partner's hands. Remind your athletes that these progressive drills were just for perfecting the technique, and that during the game they will always need to be prepared to jump and move toward the ball.

For jump headers, the players' focus is now on getting their momentum to shift from a horizontal run to a vertical jump. You can begin jump header practice by having your players perform the standing header drill again, but with the partners standing a few steps away from each other (see figure 11.4a). For this drill, the player

Figure 11.3 The athlete emphasizes an explosive two-foot take-off when heading a stationary ball from a standing position.

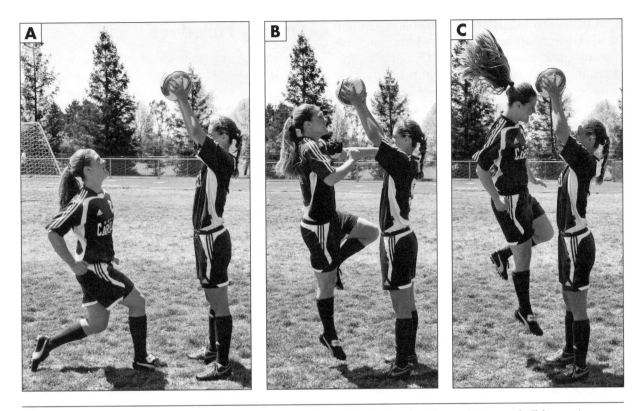

Figure 11.4 The athlete emphasizes an explosive one-foot takeoff when heading a stationary ball from a jump.

takes a short run up to the ball and uses a one-foot takeoff prior to heading the ball, which will enable her to jump higher (see figure 11.4, *b* and *c*). If the player has too much momentum going forward and not enough going up, she will either misdirect the ball, miss it completely, or crash into her partner.

After players have mastered jump heading using a stationary ball, they can progress to learning the full competitive skill of heading balls in the air in a combative environment. This takes courage, and this is where many athletes decide that they are not good in the air. As a coach, it's important to challenge your athletes and encourage them to face the things that they believe are not their strengths. Remind them that they will be faced with making these decisions in games and will continue to be discouraged if they do not commit to getting better by making the most of each training session.

To perform the competitive jump header, the player must transfer her momentum from horizontal to vertical—that is, from running to jumping. As the player moves toward the ball,

she should stay focused on the flight of the ball and not the opponent. If she is worried about the opponent, she will lose sight of the ball and her timing and alignment will suffer. Focusing on the opponent will also cause her to lose concentration on the skill she is performing.

During the jump phase, the knees should be flexed and the arms should rise slightly to help with the upward momentum. Ideally, you'll want your athletes to approach the ball with a short run-up followed by a one-foot takeoff. The one-foot takeoff allows the athlete to jump higher and contact the ball at its highest point, which is helpful when going up against an opponent. Your players will generally favor jumping off one foot over the other, but they should practice jumping off either foot so they can be successful in any tactical situation.

When players do not have the time or space for the run-up and one-foot takeoff, they will have to use a two-foot takeoff. Have them practice the two-foot takeoff, emphasizing the importance of getting in line with the ball. Explain that, aside from the jump, the rest of the technique is the same as the one-foot takeoff.

Immediately before striking the ball in a jump header, the head and shoulders bend back as a result of arching the trunk in preparation for driving through the ball (see figure 11.5a). The proper striking surface is the middle of the forehead at the hairline (see figure 11.5b). Players should head through the ball, taking on an attacking mentality, rather than letting the ball just hit the head. The striking surface stays firm as a result of keeping the neck tight and driving the forehead through the ball. The eyes are kept open, and the mouth is closed. Watching the ball allows the player to focus on hitting it either above or below the middle of the ball, depending on the tactical situation and where she wants the ball to go. Keeping her mouth closed keeps her from biting her tongue or having her teeth hit the back of an opponent's head. Also, during the strike, the head and shoulders drive forward, the arms are pulled back and raised to shoulder height, and the elbows are flexed. The arms are out wide for balance and to keep the opponent at a distance when challenging for balls in the air.

Diving Headers

The diving header is the most difficult type of header. It is used when a cross or pass is far away from the athlete and allows the player the option to finish a cross that she might otherwise miss.

A diving header can be dangerous in a crowded area because the ball is somewhere between being high enough to head and low enough to kick. Although we don't see many diving headers at the youth level, your athletes should still know how to perform this skill after practicing it in a safe and encouraging environment.

When diving to head a ball, the athlete must keep the eyes open and the head slightly tilted back with the neck tight. The timing of the dive is critical. A ball headed too early will typically rise up, whereas a ball headed too late, with the eyes down, will likely end up hitting the ground.

As the player squares the shoulders and faces the ball, she should get in a slightly crouched position just before the dive. The player pushes off with her leg to get her feet off the ground and

Figure 11.5 When performing the jump header, the athlete transfers momentum from horizontal to vertical and focuses on the flight of the ball.

dives forward so that her body is parallel to the ground (see figure 11.6*a*). Note that the takeoff is typically with one foot because the player is attempting this header off a short run up to the ball. The player then drives through the ball, continuing her momentum forward through the point of contact (see figure 11.6*b*). The player should cushion the fall with her hands and arms as she continues to move forward and lands on her trunk (see figure 11.6*c*).

Because the dive is the most difficult part of the diving header, it can be helpful to have your athletes practice the dive without the ball. Have the athletes practice diving parallel to the ground over a low hurdle, keeping their heads tilted back slightly and their necks firm. Once they are comfortable with the dive, have a partner toss a ball so that they have to jump over the hurdle to make contact. They can practice this move with cones or in front of the goal to learn how to direct the path of the ball by turning their heads slightly left or right to hit the target.

Flicked Headers

The flicked (or flick-on) header is used to change the flight of the ball while allowing it to continue in the same direction. This skill requires very little power because the athlete uses the speed of the ball while deflecting it off the center of the forehead. It is often used in front of the near post off a crossed ball or a corner kick. Deflecting the flight pattern of the ball can make reading a cross or a corner kick difficult for the goalkeeper.

When using the flicked header, the player should first make sure that the service has plenty of momentum so that she can use the speed of the ball to execute the skill. The player should then move into position to line up with the flight of the ball and use the flicked header to deflect the ball behind her, creating a new flight pattern for the ball that is difficult for the defense to read. To redirect a ball that is served low (between the chest and head), the athlete

Figure 11.6 When performing the diving header, the athlete keeps the eyes open because the timing of the dive is critical.

must bend at the knees with the trunk arched back and the chest up as she makes contact with the lower half of the ball with the upper part of her forehead (see figure 11.7a) and drops the head back to redirect the ball (see figure 11.7b). The arms should be out for balance, and the eyes should be on the ball.

To redirect a ball that is served high, the athlete must jump to meet the ball and follow the same technique as mentioned earlier (see figure 11.8, a and b). The most common mistake is not tracking the ball properly and letting it hit the middle the forehead, which sends it back in the direction it came from.

Figure 11.7 Flicked headers for a low ball require the athlete to bend at the knees and arch the trunk back. This forces the chest up and drops the head back to redirect the ball.

Figure 11.8 Flicked headers for a high ball require the athlete to jump properly and track the ball using the same technique as for a flicked header with a low ball.

HEADING ACTIVITIES

Some athletes may have to overcome an earlier experience of a painful header. It takes only one bad experience—a hard-hit ball timed incorrectly and hit in the wrong spot of the head—to shy an athlete away from heading a ball. They know they need to learn heading, and usually enjoy the drills and games that lead up to it, but when it comes time to get on the end of a driven ball, they can become less than enthusiastic. Most athletes gain confidence in their heading skills and the courage necessary to use heading in aggressive game situations through proper training. Prior to having your players practice heading, make sure the balls are properly inflated (you can even underinflate initially), or use a softer ball such as a volleyball in the beginning stages.

As you coach the skills necessary for successful heading, be sure to emphasize proper technique and make necessary corrections so your athletes establish good heading habits. Start with simple stationary drills and progress to more complex drills that require opposition and directional heading. As the athletes progress, make heading drills as gamelike as possible, allowing them to go up against other players to win balls in the air. Regardless of their position, all players should learn both defensive and offensive (attacking) headers because they will have to use both at some point in their playing careers.

The following heading drills will teach your athletes when and how to execute the correct heading techniques for a variety of tactical situations while becoming more confident on the ball.

Heading Between Cones

Objectives To provide repetition for developing various heading techniques; also improves footwork and fitness.

Description Divide players into pairs. Each pair gets one ball and three cones. They use the cones to make a playing area, placing two cones 6 yards apart and the third cone between the two cones and set back 1 yard. One player serves (S) while the other works (P). P starts at the middle cone. On your signal, she sprints to the left cone, turns around the cone, and checks to her partner (S) to receive a toss for a header. Immediately after heading, P backpedals to the middle cone, turns and sprints to the right cone, and repeats the drill until time is up. Players rotate every 30 to 60 seconds on your signal. Emphasize quick movements and sharp turns around the cones. Players should each get three rounds incorporating jump headers, driven headers, and diving headers. Servers must focus on accurate throws based on the type of header being performed.

Variations

- Include various types of runs to incorporate fitness, such as shuffles and high knees.

- Have the server call out which type of header the player should perform just before the toss.

- Add another server and working player in the same grid and have the working players start in the middle and split to opposite cones with their own servers. With two players going at once, they will have to pay attention to their runs so they do not crash into each other.

Flick-On Drill

Objectives To develop the technique for the flick-on and glancing header and practice redirecting the ball with the head.

Description Divide players into groups of four and give each group two to four balls. Within the group, players pair up and spread out 30 to 40 yards from the other pair (distance depends on the technical ability of your team; the farther apart the pairs are, the more difficult the drill). A player from one pair serves a long ball to the other pair. One player in the receiving pair tracks the ball and tries to flick it to her partner, who is behind her and slightly off to the side waiting for the flick. If the waiting partner catches the flick, she scores 1 point for her team. If the waiting partner can use her chest, thigh, or foot to receive and then catch the ball, it is worth 2 points.

The player who flicked the ball now sends a long ball to the other pair. Remember that all four players are working as a team and totaling their points. This ensures that they focus on good service and proper communication. Partners rotate among serving, flicking, and catching after each ball. Players play for 10 to 15 minutes. Before starting this drill, make sure balls are properly pumped, and do not stay on heading drills too long.

Variations

• Players can serve various types of balls based on your directive, such as low-driven, lofted, and even bended balls.

• Combine two groups and have the athletes compete to get to the flick and catch first.

Heading Competition

Objectives To develop heading with direction and pace, to practice accuracy when passing with the head, to concentrate on the transition from offense to defense, and to develop quickness and endurance.

Description Players are divided into pairs. Set up 4- × 10-yard playing areas with cones. Set up enough areas so that two groups of partners can play in each. One player on team A is positioned on the end line of the playing area, and the other is inside the area. The players on team B are positioned anywhere along the opposite end line (see figure 11.9).

Play begins with player 1 on team A (the player on the end line) tossing the ball to player 2. Player 2 can stand anywhere in the grid, but the toss must begin from the end line by player 1. After the toss, player 1 can move into the grid, and player 2 can attempt to score directly

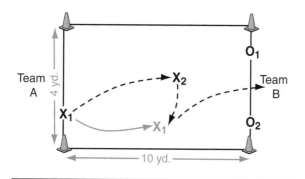

Figure 11.9 Heading Competition.

off the toss or can head the ball back to player 1, who can attempt to score. A score is made if the header crosses the end line. Players must try to score without the ball hitting the ground. If it hits the ground in the playing area during a scoring attempt, team B starts where the ball landed, and team A must hustle back to the end line to defend the header.

Players can use any body part to stop the ball, but they must be standing on the end line to defend the shot. Players may not stop a shot in the middle of the grid. If they do, the other team gets to start where they touched it. If a goal is scored, the team restarting must start the toss from the end line. Players play two- to four-minute rounds.

Variations

• Run a heading competition tournament by playing double elimination. Rotate teams with the winners staying in their grid and the losing teams rotating to their left until they've lost twice.

• Provide point penalties, such as the attacking team will be awarded a point, if a team is trying to stop the shot off the end line.

Heading Battle

Objectives To develop offensive and defensive heading techniques under pressure, and to practice timing a flighted ball.

Description Players are divided into groups of four, each of which has one ball. Two players from each group line up in the middle of the field, ready to battle for the ball. The other two players are servers and line up at the opposite penalty box (see figure 11.10). Player 1 serves a flighted ball to players 2 and 3. Player 2 tries to flick the ball to player 4 for a point (offensive header). At the same time, player 3 tries to head the ball back to player 1 (defensive header) for a point. Now players turn and face player 4, who serves a ball to players 3 and 2, and they switch roles. Now player 3 is trying to flick the ball while player 2 is trying to head the ball back to the server. Have players rotate with the servers every three to five headers.

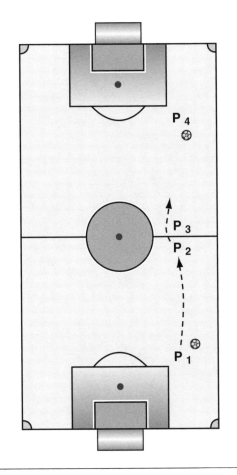

Figure 11.10 Heading Battle.

Variations

- Servers can serve various types of balls to challenge the players heading.
- Set up cones for players to head through to double their points.

CHAPTER 12 GOALKEEPING

Goalkeeping is one of the most overlooked positions on the field, and yet one of the most important. Most of us have been involved in games in which one team dominated in terms of possession and shots on goal, but went on to lose the game 1-0 because of the opposing goalkeeper's ability. Unlike field players, goalkeepers typically do not get second chances; one mistake often means a ball in the back of the net. This is just one example of why having a high-quality goalkeeper is crucial.

Goalkeepers usually handle the ball for an average of three minutes or less per game. They often go several minutes without touching the ball and then suddenly must be at the top of their mental and physical game. They are expected to remain calm and focused while reacting with precision to what could be a game-deciding situation.

To be able to deal with intense situations followed by long periods of no ball contact, today's goalkeepers must have incredible composure, self-discipline, and the psychological maturity to maintain a strong mental focus. In addition, they must be self-motivated and take responsibility for their training environment more so than players in any other position on the field. At the high school level, most teams do not have experienced goalkeeper coaches on a regular basis, so coaches must figure out a way to create training sessions for their goalkeepers.

Great goalkeepers are usually self-motivated and know how to take initiative; they have tre-mendous mental focus; they accept and own their mistakes and have the maturity to move on; they are exceptionally good at multitasking and possess excellent leadership qualities; they communicate well with their teammates, which not only helps them prevent shots, but also gives their team a sense of confidence and control; they maintain a fearless attitude in the most demanding situations; they are composed; and most important, they love their position and are incredibly passionate about the game!

GOALKEEPING TECHNIQUE

As the game of soccer has evolved, so have the demands of goalkeepers. They are required to be good not only with their hands, but also with their feet. In addition to having good catching and footwork skills, successful goalkeepers know how to dive, box, parry, distribute, and stop breakaways. Although all these skills are important, the two critical areas of focus are footwork and hands. The way a goalkeeper moves her feet will determine whether she will be in a position to make a save. However, all her footwork can be in vain if she does not know how to collect a ball properly. There are a variety of ways to move the feet and catch the ball. The successful goalkeeper trains so she can make the appropriate choice in split-second situations.

Note: This chapter was written with assistance from Kelli Robinson.

Goalkeeping Footwork

Proper footwork is the foundation for extending the female goalkeeper's mobility and range on the field. The objective is to get as much of the body behind the ball as possible, and proper footwork helps to achieve this. Proper footwork improves mobility, agility, range of coverage, and angle cutting. Great footwork makes difficult saves look easy, and often footwork is what separates average goalkeepers from great goalkeepers. Surprisingly, coaches and goalkeepers often mistakenly overlook this component in their training.

It is especially important that female goalkeepers perfect their footwork. Top female goalkeepers can be very athletic, having mastered techniques, tactics, and mind-set at the same (or higher) levels as some of the top male goalkeepers. However, genetics deals a hand, and most females at all levels lack the height and reach advantages of their male counterparts. The bottom line is that all goalkeepers, male or female, are responsible for covering 192 square feet. The speed of shots coming at goal varies from 30 to 70 miles per hour. Clearly, it takes great athleticism, sound tactics, and strong technical ability, not to mention mental toughness, to be an effective goalkeeper.

Both you and your goalkeepers should know the most commonly used footwork techniques and which ones to use in certain situations. In this section we define common footwork techniques, explain situations in which to use them, and provide excellent footwork training exercises that will improve the footwork fitness and overall ability of your goalkeepers. Following are the nine most common goalkeeper-specific footwork techniques:

1. Goalkeeper's stance
2. Lateral shuffle
3. Three-step quick start
4. Collapse step
5. Power dive step
6. Recovery drop step
7. Backpedal step
8. Crossover step
9. Vertical jump step

A Story About Choice

While playing professional soccer in Europe, I competed against a 6'2" goalkeeper with a huge reach. Despite my training, desire, and athleticism, I'm only 5'6" on my tiptoes. However, I have a lightning-quick 5'2" arm span. I was able to beat this 6'2" European giant. Why?

First, I was blessed with good genetics for strength, power, and explosive speed; hence, one of my nicknames in college was Scud Missile. Early on, I chose to make my size an advantage, so I trained hard and smart while enhancing my genetic strength, speed, and agility to conquer my height and arm span challenges. I was motivated by the fact that a coach once told me I was too short to be a goalkeeper before he even saw me play. Fortunately, my love of goalkeeping outweighed his first impression, and I went on to play goalkeeper for him and made it all the way to a professional level 15 years later!

My success was a result of my training efficiency, desire, and genetic potential. I had worked hard to develop a lot of agility, power, and strength, and a decent amount of endurance. But my greatest secret weapon was my quick footwork, something I trained at daily. I was lucky enough in my high school years to have observed a coach at a goalkeeper camp (I was the only female out of 163 goalkeepers) stress the importance of footwork. He said to a fellow camper who was power diving for every ball, "Power diving is a showman's way of hiding his lack of footwork ability." This hit home, and I began making footwork a larger part of my training. I immediately began seeing the benefits of increased range.

A tall body with an awesome reach is a great asset, but the feet are what ultimately get the hands within reach of the ball. An athlete with slow footwork, lack of efficient footwork, or poor footwork technique will have a hard time reaching her optimum potential as a goalkeeper. Footwork is the most crucial element of fitness training for all goalkeepers, short or tall.

Goalkeeper's Stance

The goalkeeper's ready stance is often referred to as a gorilla stance. It is an athletic stance that the goalkeeper should take when there is

Figure 12.1 Goalkeeper's ready stance.

a possibility of having to react to a shot or an attacking player. In this stance, the goalkeeper is squared off to the ball, the feet are slightly wider than the shoulders, and the weight is on the toes or balls of the feet (see figure 12.1). The hands are forward and ready to receive the ball, while the shoulders are rounded and the legs are slightly crouched so the keeper is ready to jump or move in any direction.

Lateral Shuffle

The goalkeeper uses the lateral shuffle to collect balls that are coming to one side or the other. In the lateral shuffle, the body moves sideways, the shoulders are square to the ball, and the feet brush smoothly across the ground (see figure 12.2, *a* and *b*). The sideways position puts the goalkeeper in a good position to step or dive quickly in any direction at a moment's notice. In some instances, crossing over will get the keeper to the ball more quickly than the lateral shuffle. However, because a goalkeeper should strive to make the save while keeping the most options open, the lateral shuffle should be her first choice.

Figure 12.2 In the lateral shuffle, the body moves sideways and the shoulders remain square to the ball.

Three-Step Quick Start

The three-step quick start is essentially three linear steps forward with the intent to cover as much ground as possible, as shown in figure 12.3, *a-c*, without overstriding, which limits agility. A goalkeeper who can explode off her line can cut down the angle of the attacking player coming to goal much more efficiently than can a goalkeeper who is slow moving off her line.

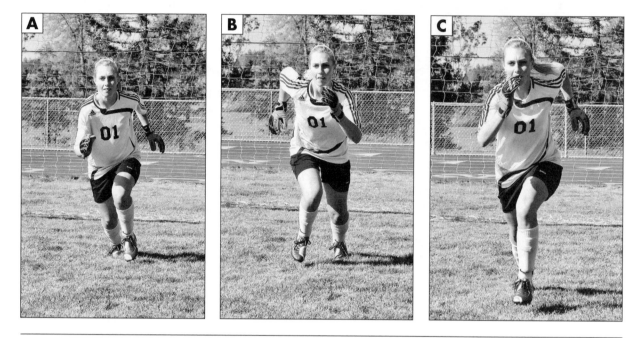

Figure 12.3   The three-step quick start allows the goalkeeper to cover more ground efficiently.

Collapse Step

A goalkeeper uses a collapse step when a ball is low and driven and very close to the side of her body, requiring her to quickly collapse her feet out from underneath her. The collapse initiates with the ankle closest to the ball. As the ankle rotates in, the knee collapses as the lower leg hits the ground first, appearing as though the goalkeeper has kicked her own legs out from under her (see figure 12.4*a*). As the hands go to the ball, the thigh hits the ground, followed by the hips (see figure 12.4*b*).

Figure 12.4   The collapse step is used for low and driven balls that are close to the goalkeeper's body.

Power Dive Step

The power dive step is used to initiate a power or extension dive, which will be discussed later on page 125. To execute the power dive step, the foot closest to the ball, known as the takeoff, or power, leg, steps forward toward the flight of the ball. As the goalkeeper coils at the hip and knee, she springs off the closest leg (see figure 12.5a). At the same time, the opposite leg, often referred to as the thrust leg, drives upward toward the direction of the ball (see figure 12.5b). It is important that the hands and head follow the movement to provide greater coverage of the ball.

Less experienced goalkeepers often have trouble getting a good, powerful takeoff. This may be a result of lack of strength and power or difficulty understanding the timing and synchronization of the movement. Keep in mind that if the head and hands do not follow the movement toward the ball, they act as an anchor preventing optimal coverage of the ball.

Recovery Drop Step

The recovery drop step is the first step in the crossover step, which will be explained later on page 119. It is the initial step back toward the goal to reach a ball that has been hit over the goalkeeper's head to one side or the other. For example, if a ball is hit toward the upper left corner of the goal (or to the goalkeeper's right side), the goalkeeper's right foot takes a step back toward the goal (see figure 12.6).

Figure 12.6 The recovery drop step is used as the first step back toward goal for a ball over the goalkeeper's head.

Figure 12.5 The power dive step is used in beginning a power or extension dive.

The placement of this step must be behind the arc of the ball so that the goalkeeper's body is between the ball and the goal when she makes contact with the ball. After the right foot takes a step back, the movement flows into a left-foot slide (see figure 12.7, *a* and *b*) or crossover (see figure 12.8), and these movement patterns are repeated as needed.

As mentioned previously, the drop step and the crossover step should be used minimally; a lateral shuffle or an explosive closing step should be used when at all possible. If goalkeepers find themselves in a lot of drop or crossover step situations they should examine their ability to read high balls and their decisions about when to come off their line.

Figure 12.7   Left-foot slide after the drop step.

Figure 12.8   Crossover to the right foot after the drop step.

Backpedal Step

The backpedal step is typically used for balls lofted directly over the goalkeeper's head. To backpedal, the goalkeeper must keep her torso slightly forward and drop the butt back and low while staying on her toes or the balls of her feet. The steps are short and light (see figure 12.9, *a-c*). The hands remain forward in a ready position to help maintain balance. Goalkeepers should choose the backpedal option over the drop crossover step whenever possible because it allows them to keep their hips and shoulders square to the play, allowing them to make quicker movement choices. Remind your athletes to maintain vision of the field and stay in the ready stance as they learn how to backpedal quickly and efficiently.

Crossover Step

The crossover step should be used as a last resort when the goalkeeper is caught well off her line and is forced to backtrack to a ball that has been hit over her head. This step should only be used when the drop or backpedal steps would not be quick enough to cover the ground needed to make the save.

To perform the crossover step, the goalkeeper starts by getting square to a ball that has been lofted high and over her left or right side. If the ball is over her right side, she initiates the crossover step with a drop step by stepping with her right leg in the direction of the ball . This is followed by the left foot and leg actually crossing over and in front of the right leg. The weight shifts to the left foot, and the right leg continues to take another drop step, followed with the left leg crossing over the right foot again.

The crossover step provides for better mobility than running back to get into position because the hips and shoulders are not completely facing away from the ball. The crossover step is quicker than the lateral shuffle or the drop step; however, it limits the keeper's ability to get the correct footing to go into a power dive, as well as her ability to change direction quickly. In addition to limiting field visibility, there is also a greater risk of getting the feet tangled while performing this step.

Figure 12.9   The backpedal step allows the goalkeeper to keep the hips and shoulders square to the play.

Vertical Jump Step

The vertical jump step is used when the ball is directly over the goalkeeper's head. The goalkeeper positions her body so the ball is directly over her head, hips, and shoulders as she squares her body to the ball. This position is the same regardless of whether the ball is coming from a shot in the front or from a cross. The vertical jump step is a one-leg takeoff that starts by rolling off the heel onto the toe. The keeper then drives the opposite knee straight upward, while simultaneously driving the hands toward the ball (see figure 12.10).

Figure 12.10 A one-foot takeoff is used for a vertical jump for balls directly over the goalkeeper's head.

Goalkeeping Hand Collections

In goalkeeping, soft, strong, quick hands are key to avoiding second-chance rebounds and keeping the net clean. Size doesn't determine great hands (although larger hands can be a slight advantage over smaller hands because they cover more surface area of the ball). Rather, a goalkeeper's fingertip strength and her ability to cushion and relax the hands and elbows are primary factors in clean collections and taking pace off the ball in intense situations.

Following are the five most common collections for goalkeepers:

1. Shovel (Scoop)
2. Cradle
3. W, or contour
4. High W, or high contour
5. Redirects

Shovel (Scoop)

The shovel, also known as the scoop, is used for collecting balls that are rolling or bouncing below the knees of the goalkeeper as she approaches the ball. As the goalkeeper prepares to catch the ball, she drops down toward the ball with her palms facing up and shoulder-width apart and her forearms parallel (see figure 12.11a). As the palms slide underneath the ball, they curl the ball into the forearms, tucking the ball up and in toward the chest and shoulders (see figure 12.11b). The shoulders should be rounded forward as the chest draws in to cushion the ball (see figure 12.11c).

Cradle

The cradle technique mirrors the shovel catch except that the shovel is used for balls on the ground and the cradle is used for balls between the knees and waist (see figure 12.12, a and b). It is important to emphasize that the shoulders roll forward to provide extra security in cushioning the ball.

Figure 12.11 The shovel is used for balls rolling or bouncing below the knees of the goalkeeper.

Figure 12.12 The cradle is similar to the shovel but is used for balls between the knees and waist of the goalkeeper.

The W, or Contour

The W, or contour, is used for chest-level or higher balls when the goalkeeper is in either a vertical or horizontal position. This grip requires the hands to be positioned in front of the body at chest height or above with the elbows and forearms parallel and perpendicular (see figure 12.13*a*). The thumbs create a W position from the back view of the hands. The hands are flexed forward slightly, creating a contour position to maximize fingertip strength and touch while providing a rock-solid grip. The head should be lined up, and the eyes should be looking through the W (or window) at the ball.

As the ball is coming toward the goalkeeper, it is crucial that she extend her arms to reach out for the ball. As the goalkeeper makes contact with the ball, the hands drop back toward the shoulders as the elbows flex in, taking pace off the ball (see figure 12.13*b*). This provides a cushioning effect, which lessens the likelihood of having to make a second save.

Figure 12.13 The W, or contour, grip is used when saving chest-level or higher balls.

The High W, or High Contour

The high W, or high contour, is used for a hard driven or lofted ball above the head, often while in a crowded situation. The high W is almost identical to the chest-high W; however, the goalkeeper must focus on keeping the hands cupped forward and over the top of the ball when she catches it. The hands must maintain a contoured, "piano-like" position, meaning that they are flexed forward at the wrist with the fingertips curved into the ball (see figure 12.14). It is important to remind the athlete that she must receive the ball at its highest point and pause slightly in the air upon making the catch. This pause allows her to avoid the ball being knocked out of her hands by an incoming, attacking player.

Redirects

Redirects are used for any ball that cannot be caught successfully. Redirecting often occurs in extreme weather conditions, crowded situations, or close-range shots and crosses when the goalkeeper realizes she cannot catch the ball cleanly. There are two types of redirects—boxing and parrying.

Figure 12.14 The high W, or high contour, is used for hard-driven or lofted balls above the head.

Boxing Boxing is a technique that can intimidate attackers and create a dominating presence for goalkeepers. Boxing is most commonly used when a goalkeeper wants to change the flight pattern of the ball for maximum height, distance, and width. One-handed boxing requires more skill and is used in extremely crowded situations in which two hands cannot get to the ball; it is typically used to clear in the same direction of the ball's flight pattern. Two-handed boxing is used to redirect a ball back where it came from. The goalkeeper should use a one-handed box only as a last resort to clear the ball out of danger. Encourage your goalkeepers to use the two-handed boxing technique over the one-handed technique when at all possible for a more controlled redirect and for better distance.

When boxing with two hands, the goalkeeper makes a flat surface by clasping her hands and resting her thumbs side by side (see figure 12.15). The wrists are close but separate, and the elbows are flexed, touching the rib cage. As the goalkeeper boxes (pushes) through the ball, she drives from the elbows for maximum height,

distance, and width. The power is generated by pushing from the chest through the bottom third of the ball.

When boxing with one hand, the same flat surface is used with the fist as mentioned previously; however, the motion is more of a quick punch with the fist as it starts from the chest area and drives through the bottom of the ball (see figure 12.16).

Figure 12.16 One-handed boxing should be used as a last resort to clear the ball.

Figure 12.15 Two-handed boxing allows for a more controlled redirect.

Parrying Parrying is used for a redirect or same-direction clearance; it is often used on shots that cannot be caught and are wide of the goalkeeper's body. The heel of the hand or the fingertips are used for the two basic types of parrying. The heel of the hand is used for parrying because it provides the strength necessary to redirect the ball away from the goal; the fingertips are used when the goalkeeper needs to push through the back side of the ball. When a shot is extremely wide, quite often the goalkeeper can only get her fingertips on the ball, which makes for an exciting save!

For both types of parrying, the goalkeeper must get her body square to the ball when setting up to parry. The heel of the active hand is facing the field and the ball, and the arm should extend at a slightly forward angle. As the hand comes toward the flight of the ball, contact is initiated at the heel of the hand as it pushes through the ball, with the fingertips leading toward the direction the keeper wants the ball to go (see figure 12.17). It is important to use the energy of the ball and push through it. Parrying a ball is often the result of a failed collapse or power dive; the goalkeeper determines she is unable to make a clean collection and must redirect the flight of the ball out of danger either around the goalpost or out of play.

Dive Saves

The goalkeeper's diving save is a top crowd pleaser because it displays athleticism and grace, often turning what was thought to be a sure goal into a miraculous save. Diligent technical training and a lot of repetition are required to master the diving save. Although the diving save is an important skill for the goalkeeper's success, it should be used only as a last resort, when a goalkeeper's footwork cannot get her directly behind the ball for a clean save. The moment a goalkeeper leaves the ground for a diving save, she risks the possibility of injury or a ball popping loose on the landing. Also, because she ends the move on the ground as opposed to standing, the chance of a quick counterattack is diminished. The diving save, although not often needed, is an integral skill to develop because it makes the impossible save possible. It should be used only as a last resort, however, and not for show.

There are three basic diving techniques:

1. Collapse dive
2. Extension (or power) dive
3. Forward dive

Collapse Dive

In the collapse dive, the goalkeeper drops and covers a low or medium ball hit slightly to her right or left. This dive is usually needed in bad weather or when the ball is struck with such velocity that the goalkeeper can't get her feet to it to make a clean save. With collapse dives, the feet usually do not leave the ground.

To execute the collapse dive on a ball hit to her right, the goalkeeper takes a step forward with her right leg (see figure 12.18a) and bends at approximately 45 degrees to the ball, allowing the foot, ankle, and leg to collapse (see figure 12.18b). The hands and head move forward to meet and cushion the ball with a side W, or contour, grip. When collapsing to the right, the right hand should be behind, but not underneath, the ball and the left hand should be on top to bring the ball down and pin it to the ground (see figure 12.18c). To avoid an unnecessary rebound, the left and right hand should meet the ball simultaneously and bring it to the ground as soon as possible, using the ground as a "third hand" of anchoring support. In the final position of the collapse dive, the goalkeeper's head and hands are behind the ball as her body forms a barrier between the ball and the goal.

The goalkeeper must make sure that she does not land on her stomach or back because this diminishes the barrier and also increases the

Figure 12.17 Parrying is used for a redirect or same-direction clearance.

Figure 12.18 The collapse dive is used when the goalkeeper can't get her feet to the ball.

chance of injury. Also, the goalkeeper should avoid landing with her elbows or arms under her chest. This can result when she tries to tuck the ball in too quickly or when she does not reach out to meet the ball.

Extension Dive

The crowd-pleasing extension dive, also called the power dive, often makes goalkeepers look superhuman when they can pull off the save (see figure 12.19). This dive to save a ball driven in the air is extremely athletic and requires a lot of technique, power, and athleticism. The extension dive is used when a ball is shot on frame (within the goalposts) and footwork alone will not allow the keeper to make the aerial save required.

The footwork leading up to the extension dive is similar to that of the collapse dive. Using the leg closest to the ball (thrust leg), the goalkeeper takes a step forward toward the ball while bending at the leg as it lowers into a coiled

Figure 12.19 The extension dive is used for balls shot on frame and driven in the air.

position. After the leg is coiled, the goalkeeper shifts her weight over the foot of the thrust leg, extending out of the coiled position as she pushes off the outside of the same foot, initiating a spring effect . The goalkeeper should drive the opposite leg (drive leg) simultaneously toward the ball with the head and hands.

When making the dive, the body should be square, behind the ball and in front of the goal. If proper synchronization occurs, the result is an explosive movement in which the goalkeeper gets off the ground to meet the ball with the hands in a side contour grip. At that point, the body creates a barrier between the ball and the goal. When landing, the ball should be first to hit the ground followed closely by the arms, shoulders, torso, and legs, providing the best shock absorption and safety for landing. Be sure your goalkeepers avoid turning forward or backward or putting their hands out to break the fall.

When training for the extension dive, choose a soft grassy area to limit possible injury. Sand pits, beaches, wrestling mats, and pole vault or high jump mats are also excellent resources.

Forward Dive

The forward dive is most commonly used for hard driven or skipping balls below the waist or in wet weather when the ball tends to be slippery and the typical shovel collection does not provide for a secure catch.

When executing the forward dive, the goalkeeper should use her footwork to approach the ball with the preferred split, or stride, step (see figure 12.20a). This provides flexibility, balance, and mobility for dealing with sudden or unexpected bounces. When the goalkeeper has positioned herself behind the ball with the shoulders squared off and the knees slightly flexed and staggered toward the ball, she then extends her hands toward the ball, palms up, pinkies close together, and slides her hands under the ball (see figure 12.20b). She flexes her wrists so the ball curls into her forearms much like the scoop technique. However, once the ball is drawn in, the momentum of the goalkeeper will continue forward as she bends at the waist and lands on her forearms, pushing through the ball. The ball will be pinned between her forearms and her chest with her legs extended and flat to the ground. This will prevent any chance of the ball slipping out.

TACTICAL AWARENESS AND RESPONSIBILITIES FOR GOALKEEPERS

Today's goalkeepers must understand the impact they have on the game. Not only do they need to be technically sound, but they must also know how to read the game, know how to organize their defense, understand their starting position, know how and when to cut off angles, be great communicators, and initiate the first

Figure 12.20 The forward dive is used for hard-driven balls below the waist.

line of attack for the team. In short, tactics comes down to decision making. Goalkeepers must make split-second decisions in situations that are continually changing. Therefore, they must practice reading the game. The better they become at recognizing cues, the better their decisions and movements will be. Looking for cues and recognizing when a shot will be taken allows the goalkeeper to get in the set position or proper stance and significantly improves her shot-saving abilities.

In addition to learning how to read the game and make quick decisions, the goalkeeper must learn to be patient and realize that making a decision too early can be a huge mistake and result in a goal. She must learn to react to situations as they develop. She also needs the courage to put pressure on the attacking player by forcing her to decide what to do. If the goalkeeper is in a good position and ready for the shot, she does everything in her power to make the attacking player commit first. The goalkeeper must be ready to take advantage of mistakes and be ready the moment the ball is shot.

Positioning

In the women's game, proper positioning is crucial. Proper positioning begins with the ball line, which is an imaginary line from the ball to the center of the goal. Factors that determine how far out the goalkeeper should come along the ball line include her experience, her ability, the game situation, and the tendencies of the opponent. Moving out along the ball line reduces the angles for the shooter, making it more difficult to score a goal. Cutting down those angles leaves less open space on both sides of the goalkeeper for the ball to pass by and into the goal. However, coming off the line can make a goalkeeper vulnerable to balls played over her head, especially if she has not determined her top angle range or how close she must be to the shooter to cover a high ball.

How far off the line a goalkeeper can play depends on several factors, particularly her reactive speed and ability to leap. Athletic female goalkeepers especially should be encouraged to come off their line aggressively to cut angles, create a strong presence, and support their team in the defensive third of the field. Goalkeepers with good starting positions and

the ability to win through balls can change the way their opponents play as well as provide good attacking support for their teams, allowing the defense the confidence to push up and support the attack. When the goalkeeper plays aggressively high up the field, the opponent has difficulty playing balls behind the defense. It forces them to serve balls into areas of the field that are less dangerous, which is a good thing for your team!

Starting positions vary based on the goalkeeper's ability and experience. Whereas one goalkeeper can play farther off her line because of her size and physical ability, another may need to play closer to her goal line. A general guideline for positioning is that when the ball is in the attacking third of the field, the goalkeeper should position herself near the top third of the penalty box; when the ball is in the middle third of the field, she should be between the 6- and 12-yard marks; when the ball is in the defensive third, the goalkeeper should be close to her line and in position to deal with a shot. Note that there are situations in which the goalkeeper is not on the ball line, such as corner kicks, certain set plays, and crossed balls. In these situations the goalkeeper may need to creep off her line and go to where the ball is being played.

Angle Play

To help goalkeepers understand the concept of cutting off angles, as mentioned in the previous section, you can create a triangle by tying ropes to each end of the goalposts and extending the ropes out to meet the ball. The closer the goalkeeper gets to the ball, the closer the lines (ropes) get to her body, diminishing shooters' options. This positioning allows the athlete to maintain an equal position from either post when the shot is taken. When a goalkeeper stays on her line, she not only gives up a large portion of the penalty box, but also gives the attacking player a huge target to shoot at. By coming out toward the ball and cutting off the angle, the goalkeeper has significantly cut down the size of the goal and limits the attacker's shooting options.

It is important for the goalkeeper to recognize that the farther she steps off her line, the more she needs to understand her top angle positioning to avoid balls being chipped over her head. To create a visual that shows how to decrease the area a ball can be chipped over the head, you can tie a third rope to the middle of the cross bar and bring it down to meet the ball. This will show the goalkeeper in various positions where she is vulnerable on the top angle when stepping out to cover the side angles.

Three-Goal Situation

The three-goal situation develops when the opponent has beaten the defender up the flank. As the attacking player enters the penalty box, the goalkeeper's first priority is to prepare for a shot on goal and cover the near post (first goal). It is the goalkeeper's responsibility to prevent a goal at the near post!

The next concern for the goalkeeper is a ball that is played from the flank on the ground between her and the six-yard box. This is considered the second goal opportunity in the three-goal situation. If the ball gets past the goalkeeper to an approaching attacking player, that player has a fairly easy shot on goal. The goalkeeper's job is to cut off the pass in the hope of avoiding an open goal situation. She must do whatever she can to keep the ball away from any attacking player in front of the goal. The goalkeeper must know her positional priorities as she is covering the near post while positioning herself to win the (second goal) ball.

The last priority for the goalkeeper (third goal) is to cover a ball that is played over her head to the far post. The goalkeeper's communication skills are necessary because she must organize a defender to cover that space and compete for the ball. The goalkeeper must remain patient in the three-goal situation and remember her priorities. Even if the back post has an open attacking player, the near post is always her first responsibility. The goalkeeper's position needs to be strong so that the attacking player thinks she cannot score at the near post (first goal). When the attacking player's head goes down, the goalkeeper can move out a bit to begin covering the pass that is played into the front of the goal and prevent a scoring opportunity.

Breakaways (1v1s)

The breakaway save requires proper technique and timing and takes a tremendous amount of courage. Breakaway situations occur when a ball has been played behind the defense to an attacking player, or when an attacking player has dribbled through the defense and is approaching the goalkeeper in a 1v1 situation. Proper positioning and timing are key in stopping a breakaway. If the goalkeeper leaves from a bad spot (out of position) or leaves too early, she can find herself stranded and leaving an open goal for the attacker.

The main objective in a breakaway is for the goalkeeper to win the ball before the shot is taken. As the attacking player advances, the goalkeeper must come out under control (stealing ground) and wait for the chance to win the ball outright. It is important for the goalkeeper to approach the ball at the same pace as the incoming attacker. In other words, if the attacker is coming in slowly, the goalkeeper should approach slowly. If the attacker is moving in quickly, the goalkeeper must match that pace. As the goalkeeper moves toward the attacker, she must be ready to "smother" the ball the moment it is overplayed (touched too far in front of the body), getting to the ball before the attacker can get another touch.

When the goalkeeper and attacker meet the ball at the same time, the goalkeeper must go in hard and low with the hands leading to protect her face and head. As the attacker is striking the ball, the goalkeeper's forearms absorb the shot. The ball is caught with the wrists bent, while the hands go around the outside of the ball. The goalkeeper must stay on her feet as long as possible. Once she is on the ground, she is committed and has a very small chance of getting up in time to make a second save.

When an attacking player has total control of the ball and it's too late for the goalkeeper to come crashing out, the goalkeeper must position herself to deal with a shot by staying upright and making herself look as big as possible. As the attacker approaches, the goalkeeper should keep her body weight forward and remain patient. When a goalkeeper must stand a player up in this way, her confidence and presence in the goal box are key to her success.

Communication is very important during a breakaway; the goalkeeper must make her intentions to her teammates very clear. Shouting "keeper" lets her chasing defender know that she is attempting to win the ball. Now the defender can continue running to the goal line to support the goalkeeper. Once the goalkeeper makes the decision to come out for a ball, she should not hesitate or change her mind midway; she's committed, and it's an all-or-nothing situation!

Distribution

The goalkeeper is the last line of defense, but the first line of attack. After making a save, she must make a decision about where the counterattack should begin. The two main types of distribution are throwing and kicking, and which one to use depends on the situation.

Kicks

A goalkeeper has essentially two choices if she decides to kick—a punt or a drop kick. The punt is used for distance, but because it has a high flight trajectory (or hang time in the air), it is not recommended for a quick counterattack. For the punt, the goalkeeper should hold the ball in the same hand as the kicking foot (see figure 12.21a). Using a short run (two or three steps) at a slight angle in the direction of the kick, the keeper points the plant foot toward the target, drops the ball out of the hand, and kicks it (see figure 12.21b). The follow-through should be straight as she lands on the kicking foot (see figure 12.21c).

In the drop kick, the goalkeeper drops the ball and kicks it after it hits the ground. It has a lower flight trajectory and therefore gets to the intended target more quickly than a punted ball, making the drop kick a good choice for quick counterattacks. This type of kick is also easier for teammates to receive because of the lower flight pattern. The technique is similar to the punt except for the timing required to strike it after the bounce. Contact should be made early just as the ball is coming off the ground (see figure 12.22, a and b). Because the drop kick requires a lot of time and practice to master, it is not as consistent as the punt.

Figure 12.21 The punt is used for distance and height.

Figure 12.22 The drop kick has a lower trajectory and should be used for quick counterattacks.

Throws

Throws are used for shorter, more accurate distribution. There are three main types of throws: the bowling, or rolling, throw; the baseball throw; and the sling, or overhand, throw. Some goalkeepers create their own versions of these throws. Regardless of the type of throw the goalkeeper decides to use, she should remember these guidelines: If her teammate is standing still, she should play the ball directly to her feet; if her teammate is running, she should lead her with the pass and try to serve it to her lead foot.

The bowling, or rolling, throw is used for short distances, typically around the 18-yard box. Because the ball is on the ground and moving at a slower pace, it is easy for teammates to receive. The disadvantages are the slow pace and the limited distance the ball can be rolled. When bowling, the goalkeeper should first get low by bending at the knees and hips. Then, she should step with the opposite foot and roll the ball, making sure the palm is facing up on the follow-through (see figure 12.23).

The baseball throw looks just like it sounds, as shown in figure 12.24. It is used for faster distribution and greater distance than the roll or bowl, and it is easily controlled by the receiver as long as it bounces before reaching its target. This type of throw is used frequently, but may

Figure 12.23 The bowling, or rolling, throw is used for short distances and accuracy.

be difficult for younger goalkeepers because the ball may slip out of their smaller hands.

The sling, or overhand, throw is the longest and often the least accurate of the throws. It is also typically a difficult throw to learn. The ball is controlled between the palm and forearm with the wrist bent, and the arm is brought back and over the head. The goalkeeper then steps in the direction of the throw and fully extends the arm with the elbow locked (see figure 12.25a). As she releases the ball, the back leg comes forward (same leg as the throwing arm), and

Figure 12.24 The baseball throw is used for faster distribution and greater distance.

the hand finishes by pointing toward the target (see figure 12.25*b*). When released correctly, the ball should have some backspin, making it easier to receive.

Communication

An ability to communicate effectively is perhaps the most important skill a goalkeeper can possess. Effective communication distinguishes a great goalkeeper from a good one. Most goalkeepers playing at higher levels rate their performances based on how many shots were taken on goal, rather than on how many they saved. A goalkeeper who communicates early and with confidence can organize her teammates and place them in the tactical advantage to stop an attack before a shot is ever taken.

It is important for the goalkeeper to communicate with her team because she is the last line of defense and the only player who faces the field for the entire game. She is in the best position to see the play develop and give helpful information and specific directions to help her defense stop an otherwise organized attack. To be successful at this, the goalkeeper must be a student of the game and know the following:

- Team defensive philosophy (so she can organize within those guidelines when possible)
- Strengths and weaknesses (tendencies) of the opposing team
- Specific role of each defender

Figure 12.25 The sling, or overhand, throw is the longest of the throws but the least accurate.

- Roles and tendencies of the forwards (to generate a successful counterattack)

The goalkeeper who takes on this degree of responsibility will find she is making fewer saves with her hands and more with her voice. Following are a few guidelines for effective communication:

- *Simplicity.* The goalkeeper must use "strong words" and avoid lengthy sentences. She should explain her terminology in training sessions so her teammates understand exactly what she wants. Team-friendly terminology will help avoid misunderstandings during intense moments in a game. For example, when the goalkeeper yells "keeper," she means she is going for the ball and that the defender should get out of her way.

- *Specificity.* The goalkeeper must tell specific players what to do. For example, she should not say, "Let's go, A. J.," but rather, "A. J., close number 10," or "Chingy, contain," or "M. J., time, turn." These specific instructions, short and to the point, tell the players exactly what to do.

- *Clarity.* The goalkeeper must avoid slurring and fast chatter. Again, no long sentences; the fewer words, the better. She should practice being loud, clear, and concise.

- *Tone.* The goalkeeper must learn to remain calm when giving instructions to give her teammates a sense of confidence and reassurance. If she sounds panicked, the defense will pick up on this right away, and tension will begin to build. She should change her tone based on the urgency of the situation. If her teammates don't hear her directions the first time, she may have to take a firmer tone the second time. Defenders should not take this tone personally; they need to understand that the goalkeeper must do whatever she can to keep the ball out of the back of the net.

- *Timing.* Goalkeepers must learn to communicate early! This gets better with tactical maturity. The goalkeeper should focus on the player with the ball first and organize the defensive players that are around the ball. Once those defenders are set, she can organize the defenders who are farther from the ball. These instructions must happen early, as the attack from the opposing players begins to build. The goalkeeper will find herself in trouble if she waits too long.

GOALKEEPER TRAINING

In addition to training your goalkeeper in the technical and tactical aspects of the game, you should also train her in the physical and psychological dimensions. Your goalkeeper's fitness needs are different from those of the field players. Although you should expect your goalkeeper to have an aerobic fitness base, it should not be the emphasis. Consider the types of movements a goalkeeper must perform as discussed in the preceding technical section. She must be able to move quickly forward, backward, and laterally, and to go down quickly and get up quickly. She has to jump, dive, shuffle, and use crossover steps. Therefore, your goalkeeper training plan should be position specific to develop her anaerobic base and the physical qualities necessary to be a successful goalkeeper.

Also, the psychological side of the goalkeeper's game should not be overlooked. Most goalkeepers tend to be very critical of themselves. As a result, letting go of mistakes can be difficult, resulting in diminished confidence. You play an important role in helping your goalkeeper develop mental skills by providing a training environment that helps her develop the composure and confidence necessary to thrive in demanding game situations. Ironically, most goalkeepers spend 90 percent of their time training physically, for a position that is 90 percent tactical and mental!

Physical Training

Superior fitness is vital especially for the female goalkeeper given her height and reach challenges. Although a large part of a goalkeeper's success depends on her mind-set and technical and tactical game, a high level of fitness is also crucial. Comparing the fitness demands of a goalkeeper to those of a field player is like comparing a sprinter to a distance runner in track and field. Specificity of training is crucial for helping any athlete achieve her true physical potential within her sport.

Although goalkeepers typically don't handle the ball for the majority of the game, they must be physically prepared to cover a goal that is 192 square feet, standing 8 feet high and 24 feet wide, while collecting balls shot on goal at a speed ranging from 30 to 70 miles per hour. Recent studies suggest that the keeper makes approximately 13 saves or cross collections and spends approximately 12 minutes of intense physical activity involving short multidirectional jumps and sprints ranging from four to five meters, all within a 90-minute game.

Because the goalkeeper position demands short bursts of all-out activity usually lasting between 0 and 30 seconds, training should focus on the anaerobic training system. The anaerobic training system does not require oxygen to function and is used during short-duration and high-intensity exercise usually lasting between 0 and 180 seconds. A large portion of goalkeeper fitness training should focus on developing goalkeeper-specific anaerobic capacity for 0 to 60 seconds at full intensity. Incorporate the following top five categories:

1. Reactive speed
2. Quickness
3. Agility
4. Power/strength
5. Short-distance speed (6-12 yards)

Reactive Speed

Reactive speed is the ability to recognize and react to a situation as soon as possible. Training reactive speed using various visual, kinesthetic, and auditory cues should rate high on the physical training list for goalkeepers. Visual or auditory commands can easily be used in goalkeeper-specific footwork drills that incorporate ladders and cones. A rubber dog toy with knobs is a great tool for developing reactive hand speed. A blindfold can be used to develop kinesthetic reaction time. For example, you can blindfold the goalkeeper and have her try to catch a ball only after she feels it touch her. This helps her develop reactive speed and kinesthetic sense in reference to touch. This

drill simulates a crowded situation in which she has lost sight of the ball but still must make the save.

Quickness

Quickness is the ability to generate movement in a short amount of time and rates a close second on the goalkeeper-specific fitness list. Most coaches will choose a quick goalkeeper or player over a fast goalkeeper or player any day. A goalkeeper who can quickly explode off her line and close down danger is more valuable than a goalkeeper who is faster but takes 10 yards to get moving. Hand quickness activities, line drills, and ladder drills involving explosive movements over a short period of time are ideal for developing quick feet for the goalkeeper.

Agility

Agility is the ability to change direction without the loss of speed, body control, or balance. Agility training should be on the priority list for all athletes, but especially goalkeepers. You may have a goalkeeper with excellent reactive skills who can see the player shooting the ball quickly and is quick to move into position for the shot; however, defenders often step in and deflect the ball in the opposite direction. Your goalkeeper will need the agility necessary to change direction rapidly to cover the shot. She can work on her own on simple drills that emphasize agility. For example, she could stand at a cone, toss a ball straight up, shuffle to another cone four yards away, touch it, and then make the save before the second bounce.

Power

Power is defined as strength over time. Goalkeepers need power to propel their bodies in several acrobatic, jumping movements and diving saves. Power is needed when footwork and speed have not gotten the job done. Power allows the goalkeeper to jump high, dive far, and get where she needs to be with explosive movements. Goalkeeper-specific plyometrics are important exercises to use in training to develop power. Such exercises include bounds, hops, jumps, and medicine ball training in which maximum effort is expended. Upper-body power and strength is also needed to ensure that the goalkeeper can hold on to shots and crosses in crowded situations.

Short-Distance Speed

Short-distance speed is the ability to move fast over a 6- to 15-yard distance, and developing it should be an important part of the goalkeeper's training. Short-distance speed is needed when a goalkeeper must come off her line to close down an attacker, get to a ball that falls behind the defense, or come out of her box to clear the ball. Short-distance speed can be worked on alone or with a partner; the only limits are the imagination. For example, the goalkeeper can begin a drill by lying on her side with the ball as though she has just made a save. She throws the ball approximately six yards away, reloads as quickly as possible, and sprints to make the breakaway save.

Eighty to ninety percent of a goalkeeper's fitness training should incorporate, but not be limited to, the top five categories listed earlier. It is also important to touch on aerobic training components to build a base fitness level, as well as to train mental toughness. Goalkeepers will also feel more connected with the field players if they take part in aerobic training sessions with the rest of the team. This encourages team bonding.

Psychological Training

The psychological traits necessary to become a great goalkeeper make the position one of the most demanding on the field. As the last line of defense, the goalkeeper's mistakes are final. Great goalkeepers must find ways to recover from, and learn to not dwell on, those mistakes. Goals are going to be scored, and the goalkeeper (as well as her teammates) must learn how to stay positive and put mistakes behind her.

You can help your goalkeeper stay positive after a goal is scored on her. If the goal is the result of her error, encourage her to quickly assess the mistake and then let it go. Using positive self-talk is a good start. Remind her, too, that not all goals are the result of a mistake. If the opponent put together a great attack with an exceptional shot, she should recognize it and then focus on staying positive while motivating the team.

Be sure to give your goalkeeper credit for doing a good job in situations other than direct saves. Maybe she forced a forward to shoot too early, or came off her line for a ball played over the defense. Acknowledging such actions helps to reinforce the importance of owning the box and gives her the confidence to play assertively. Help your goalkeeper develop good habits, just as you would your field players.

Also, be careful about pulling a goalkeeper out of a game after she's made a mistake. This could destroy her confidence and may be difficult for her to recover from. If your goalkeeper thinks you do not have confidence in her abilities, her attitude and mental toughness could decline fast! If you do have to pull her out of the game, don't instantly point out all her mistakes. Let her know it's not her day, and then address the mistakes in a positive way during the next training session.

GOALKEEPING ACTIVITIES

Even though coaches may understand the importance of the goalkeeper position, many overlook training their goalkeepers for two reasons: They don't believe they have the time because they are organizing training sessions for 20-plus field players, or they don't have the knowledge and expertise to train goalkeepers correctly. Either way, thinking that just because you've run a shooting drill you've provided training for your goalkeeper is a big mistake. If you cannot get an assistant goalkeeper coach to work with your goalkeepers, you must take it on yourself to research and use videos and training guides, in addition to taking goalkeeper courses to help you plan appropriate training sessions for them. It is important that you take the time to connect with your goalkeepers and make them feel that they are an integral part of your team's success. They will believe they are just as worthy as the field players if you take the time to plan training sessions for them.

The following goalkeeping drills will teach your athletes when and how to execute the correct goalkeeping techniques for a variety of tactical situations while becoming more confident on the ball.

Danish Corners

Objectives To develop goalkeeper communication and direction of defense in corner kicks, improve game pace shots in crossed situations, and improve the ability to generate the first attack.

Description Divide the group into teams of five with goalkeepers (GK) in each net. Set up a playing area with two standard-size goals, one on the end line and the other 30 to 36 yards out, directly across from the first goal. Use normal field sidelines for width. Mark out a penalty box for the second goal, so both goalkeepers have a proper size penalty box (they will overlap in a 30-yard area). Four players from each team position inside the area (X and O) to play 4v4. The remaining player from each team acts as a server (S); servers stand at opposite corners where a typical corner kick would be taken and have 6 to 10 balls each (see figure 12.26).

This drill focuses on shooting to provide the goalkeepers with as much repetition as possible. Corner kicks are taken for all restarts including goal kicks, throw-ins, after a goal is scored, and any corner earned. Essentially, every situation in which you would maintain possession after the ball leaves the field of play will be a corner kick. This is a very fast-paced drill; all players must transition quickly to prepare offensively and defensively for corners. It is a fun and productive drill for both field players and goalkeepers. Players play approximately 10 minutes (rotating servers every five minutes), and then rotate teams.

Variations

- Restrict the time frame for taking corner kicks to five seconds to focus on quick transitions.
- Allow more time to focus on defensive and attacking setups.

Goalkeeper Wars

Objectives To develop proper footwork and saving techniques with a variety of shots; to develop quickness, focus, and endurance; and to practice distribution technique, cutting down angles, and getting set.

Description Place two standard goals approximately 18 yards apart and divide the space between the goals in half with cones. Place a goalkeeper (GK) in each goal. Each goalkeeper should have a supply of balls on the right goalpost and a server (S) to give her a ball when ready to keep the game moving quickly (see figure 12.27). Play begins with one goalkeeper throwing, drop-kicking, volleying, or shooting the ball to attempt to score on the other goalkeeper. Each goalkeeper must stay on her

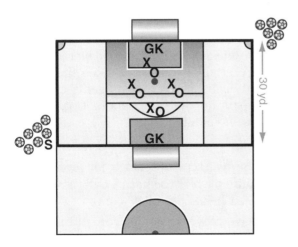

Figure 12.26 Danish Corners.

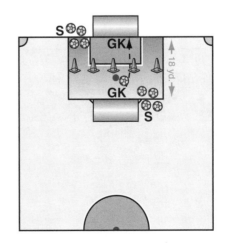

Figure 12.27 Goalkeeper Wars.

half of the grid. If the attempt goes wide or in the back of the net, the defending goalkeeper gets a ball from her server and now attempts a shot. If a save is deflected into the other half, the goalkeeper who took the shot gets a second attempt. Once the goalkeeper has control of the ball, she must shoot from where she made the save. Play continues for a set amount of time or a predetermined number of goals.

Variation

- Include field players to challenge the goalkeepers.

Train the Keeper

Objectives To develop the goalkeeper's ability to cover close-range shots, cut off crosses, cover long-range shots, communicate, organize the defense, position herself, and own the box.

Description Choose three players for shooting close-range shots and spread them out between 12 and 18 yards from the goal line with four balls each. Place two defenders (with vests) in the 6-yard box with three attacking players. The rest of the team makes an arc outside the penalty box with one or two balls each (see figure 12.28). Play begins with a cross from the first player in the arc. The three attacking players work to score against the goalkeeper and her two defenders. As soon as the ball is out of

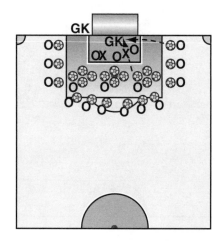

Figure 12.28 Train the Keeper.

bounds or in the back of the net, a shot comes from the first shooter lined up 12 yards from the goal line. Play continues in this pattern, with the goalkeeper dealing with a cross or long-range shot followed by an immediate close-range shot. The two defenders must work closely with the goalkeepers and position themselves properly based on the shot, the cross, or directions from the goalkeeper. In addition, the three attackers must frame the goal properly based on the shot or cross. Once all players on the arc have taken two shots, rotate players into different spots. Switch goalkeepers after each full round.

Variations

- Change the numbers of defenders and attacking players in the box.
- Allow the three attacking players to keep the ball in play by passing back to a player in the arc or to a shooter.

Rapid Fire

Objectives To develop reaction time and shot-saving techniques with shots that are fired repetitively with little time to get set.

Description The field players line up and spread out along the outside of the penalty box. Each field player has a ball at her feet and her back to the goal. A goalkeeper is in the net. Begin play by approaching the first player with a ball and passing it between her feet as she turns and takes a shot. The goalkeeper must react and defend each shot. Continue to move down the line quickly until each player has taken a shot. After all players have taken shots, they collect their balls and quickly get back in line and prepare for their next shots. Goalkeepers switch after each full round.

Variations

- Vary the type of service; for example, require players to shoot a ball tossed over their heads or volley a shot.
- Have players pass to you and turn and shoot on your pass back.
- Have players switch feet when taking shots.

Part IV

COACHING TACTICS AND SYSTEMS

CHAPTER 13 PRINCIPLES OF TEAM PLAY

Fans from around the world describe soccer as "the beautiful game." They love the game for its momentum, rhythm, and movement. Teams flow in and out of attack and defense as 11 players combine their individual efforts into a team effort and style that fits their collective personalities (as we will learn more about in chapter 14). Although you may prefer one style of play over another, you cannot determine what is best for your team until you understand the qualities your team possesses. A team's style will develop over time and will ultimately be affected by players' individual technical skills, their understanding of the game, and their positional responsibilities, as well as their fitness levels and psychological makeup.

To help you understand the principles of team play, this chapter focuses on basic attacking and defending principles, in addition to set plays. Understanding these concepts and knowing your players will help you make an informed decision when determining your team's style and system of play.

As mentioned before, you should not force a style or system on your team. To develop chemistry and cohesion within your team, include your athletes in the decision-making process. Much time will be devoted to implementing and improving your style and system of play. For your team to improve and embrace these choices, they must have a basic understanding of the concepts in this chapter while they work on their individual and technical goals. Communication and feedback between coaches and players throughout the season is vital for personal and team growth. If teammates cannot or will not work together, then team success will suffer regardless of individual talent.

ATTACKING AND DEFENDING PRINCIPLES

Understanding attacking and defending principles will not only help you get the most out of your players, but will also help you coach against any system your opposition may play against you. These principles apply regardless of your chosen system or systems and will be a part of the game indefinitely.

Attacking Principles

The first and most important principle in soccer is that ball possession is everything. Certainly, teams must sometimes risk losing possession because of goal-scoring chances. In addition to creating those chances, maintaining possession and moving the ball forward into your attacking third are attacking principles that apply when your team has the ball.

Successful attacking combinations stem from the following important aspects of attacking principles: width, support, mobility, creativity, and penetration.

Width and Support

Great attacking teams spread out their opponents' defense to create opportunities to penetrate using creative runs and passes. This is initiated by maintaining good attacking shape, staying wide, and moving the ball to outnumber the opponent or by attacking quickly in transition. In addition, an attacking movement with depth and support gives the player with the ball a variety of passing options. The number of support players is critical. As a general guideline, two players should be supporting the athlete with the ball, forming a triangle shape. A minimum of three players is needed to truly provide depth in the attack. This triangle shape can point in any direction and will often change quickly. Players must be taught that their angle of support and distance of support are areas of concern because a flat attack produces flat or square passes, which are easy to intercept.

Mobility and Creativity

Mobility and creativity are also key components of a successful attack. Although you want your players to have a plan of established attacking patterns, you also want to encourage them to read and react to each situation as it arises.

One way attacking players can disturb a defense is to constantly change positions and types of runs. Diagonal and overlapping runs can accomplish this, forcing the defense to deal with different opponents coming into their zone. If the defense is marking man to man, then the situation for the attacker is even better because the defenders have to chase a player down from one side of the field to the other. With these types of runs, the defenders are not sure whether players are moving to receive a pass or to take them out of position to make room for another attacker. If these runs are happening near or within the penalty area, then the defense has cause for concern and must focus on tracking all runs. Encourage your players to take on and beat opponents 1v1. Attack-minded players will revel in the freedom to have this opportunity to move and be creative with the ball.

Penetration

To experience success in their attack and learn to penetrate the gaps between defenders, your players must understand the various roles required of them based on the attacking principles. With a basic understanding of these roles, players have an easier time understanding the concepts of shape and space. Your athletes will learn how to see shape (diamond or triangle) developing within the buildup and make informed decisions regardless of the system or style of play they are using. As mentioned earlier, three players are needed to provide depth in the attack.

The first attacker (the player with the ball) should look to penetrate by moving the ball forward either by shooting (and ideally scoring), dribbling past a defender (creating space behind her for supporting players to run into), or passing through a gap in the defense to a supporting player. These decisions are based on where the athlete is on the field and what kind of pressure the defense is putting on her. The role of the second attacker is to provide support from various distances while creating depth and width. The second attacker is fairly close to the first attacker and must make herself available to receive a pass, create combination plays, or make penetrating runs. The second attacker also helps support the first attacker by moving away from her, drawing a second defender, and staying in constant communication.

The third attacker is farther from the player with the ball (first attacker), but still provides support for the first and second attackers. This is accomplished by making forward, penetrating runs into space and creating space by pulling defenders away from the player with the ball. Her movements should provide mobility, depth, and width and should help in balancing the shape of the attack by continuing to support the diamond shape throughout the field.

DEFENDING PRINCIPLES

The basic principles of defense are pressure, cover, and balance, regardless of where the ball is on the field. Organized defenses become concentrated and compact while limiting the amount of space and time the opposition has to work in. Defensive players must focus on the attacking players, but also the space between them, making it difficult for the opponent to penetrate with a pass through the defense. Because penetration is a huge factor in the attack, delaying with immediate pressure should remain a priority.

Like attackers, defenders should also cover for one another by forming triangular (diamond) shapes or formations. The closer the defense backs up to its own goal, the tighter those shapes become. As attackers try to get through, around, and over the top of defenders, defenders must learn to maintain coverage by staying balanced at all times. When a team loses possession, every player must be thinking and moving defensively while trying to regain possession.

Defensive players must be patient and mindful of their responsibilities and not just react to the movement of the ball. Great defensive teams show restraint by challenging and leaving their shape only when they know they can win the ball, or when they have the coverage and balance needed from their teammates. The closer the ball gets to the penalty box, the more control the defending team must have. The following sections discuss the roles players have in following the basic defensive principles of pressure, cover, and balance.

Pressure

The attacking player with the ball is the defense's first priority (first attacker) because she is the most dangerous. The defensive player closest to the ball (first defender) has the responsibility of putting pressure on the ball and should consider doing the following depending on where she is on the field:

- Reduce space by pressuring quickly.
- Win the ball or delay penetration by making the attacker slow down or turn back.
- Make play predictable by forcing the attacker to go one way.
- Deny penetrating passes through the defense.
- Tackle and win possession when she has supporting defenders around her.
- Remain patient and in control at all times.

Cover

The role of the second defender is to provide support for the first defender. The second defender should be 8 to 15 yards from the defender who is applying pressure on the ball. The second defender should communicate with the first defender and keep her aware of what is happening as play develops. The second defender's primary responsibilities are also based on where she is on the field; she should do the following:

- Support quickly and help make play predictable by getting into good supporting angles and denying penetrating passes.
- Try to maintain and keep the gap consistent between herself and the first defender. The closer they are to their penalty box, the smaller the gap should be (i.e., they should stay compact).
- Be aware of having to mark supporting attackers and be prepared to double-team the player with the ball, or pressure the second attacker who is receiving the pass.
- Help balance out the defensive shape by denying passing lanes.

Balance

The third defender provides a supporting role to the first and second defenders. Her primary responsibility is to maintain depth and balance by focusing on whether the player with the ball is about to play a long ball over the top of and behind the defense. She should also do the following:

- Read and communicate if the point of attack is going to change with a long or switched ball.
- Track players who are making forward runs.
- Take away space by anticipating and stepping into passing lanes.
- Prepare to balance the defense and be prepared to become the first or second defender as play develops.

SET PLAYS

Dead-ball situations are considered any circumstance in which the ball is put back into play after a stop in the action. Most coaches and players call them set plays, or set pieces; they include throw-ins, corner kicks, kickoffs, goal kicks, direct or indirect free kicks, and penalty kicks. Because goals can be difficult to come by in soccer, it is worth the time to practice dead-ball situations and give your team the opportunity to increase goal-scoring chances.

Your team should decide what combinations of set plays to use once you have explained their options. Their choices should be based on their abilities. For example, if you have a player who can perform a long throw-in, then the team will want to spend time working on throw-in combinations that use this skill. Once you have analyzed your talent and made specific choices about the plays you'll use, you'll need to decide which players will be primarily responsible for executing these plays. These players must have the opportunity to rehearse these plays in practice to perfect the movement and timing of the set piece. Start with the players involved in the set plays and gradually add defenders; then train in full game situations.

Players practicing dead-ball situations must concentrate on perfecting the plays. Because the process can be slow moving and not physically demanding, you may want to incorporate these plays before or after your regular training time. When the involved players and the backups know what they are doing, include the remainder of the team so there are no surprises and they understand their role in the set plays.

Finally, put your athletes in full-pressure situations in which they must make choices about which plays to use in a given situation. Your athletes' attitudes toward set plays will reflect the coaching staff's attitudes. If your athletes help make choices about the plays they'll be running, have adequate practice time in which to gain confidence in their performance, and experience success in their plays, they will be more willing to put in the concentrated effort necessary for becoming successful in dead-ball situations.

We've discussed the importance of practicing set plays and having organized attacks. It is equally important to rehearse the defensive coverage of set plays. Your team should spend time preparing defensively for all set-play situations so they are not caught off guard when faced with a play they have not seen before. No doubt you have your own beliefs and strategies for defending set plays; however, there are some standard guidelines you must understand and teach your players. Your team should have a thorough understanding of the following fundamental rules when setting up a wall:

- The goalkeeper should decide who is in the wall, but players in the wall will typically be midfielders and forwards.

- Always put one player immediately on the ball to delay a quick restart.

- Remember that most attacking pieces will be organized to pull the defense apart. Attacking players will line up where they want the defense to be; players should not be fooled into poor coverage.

- The tallest player should be in line with the post; the rest of the players should line up from the tallest to the smallest from that first player.

- A midfielder or striker can assist the goalkeeper in setting the wall, but she must communicate quickly. The goalkeeper has the ultimate say.

- Set the wall up approximately 8 to 9 yards from the ball; do not give the opponent any extra yards. The official will push the wall back to the appropriate spot, if necessary.

- Players should connect arms. One player faces the goalkeeper so she can listen to and make eye contact with the goalkeeper to be sure the wall is following her directions.

- The wall should break only if two or more passes are made; otherwise, a separate player should be designated to go to the ball as soon as it is touched.

- Players in the wall should not move, duck, or jump; they should stay in place!

- On corner kicks, coverage can be a combination of man-to-man and zone, but the bottom line is that players have a responsibility to get to the ball!

- Defenders sprinting out after the ball is played must be ready to hold and stop if the opposition wins the ball back.

CHAPTER 14 SYSTEMS OF PLAY

Most coaches have their favorite systems of play, but all coaches should understand the strengths and weaknesses of the various systems so they can make the best tactical decisions for their teams. Systems of play, or team formations, indicate how individual players are positioned based on the three zones of a soccer field: defensive zone, midfield, and attacking zone. These systems are identified by number combinations within each zone. For example, a 4-4-2 would indicate four defenders, four midfielders, and two attackers. A team's chosen formation is used as a guideline to help the athletes support each other in their attacking and defending strategies. For many, it is a given that each formation begins with a goalkeeper, but more recently, formations list the goalkeeper, recognizing that position as part of the system. Now, formations are described as 1-4-4-2, for example, rather than just 4-4-2, to include the goalkeeper. (The formations covered in this chapter are identified in this manner.)

SELECTING A SYSTEM

The system of play you choose should fit your athletes' overall abilities, taking into consideration their ages, fitness levels, and technical and tactical abilities. You should also consider your athletes' knowledge of their responsibilities within a system, as well as how your opposition plays. Every system has advantages and disadvantages that you should fully understand before deciding what's right for your team. Consider these along with your athletes' and team's strengths and weaknesses. Taking the time to learn as much as you can about each formation, getting your athletes' input, and understanding your athletes' abilities can help you make an informed decision that supports your program's goals and vision. Be mindful of your own expectations, and remember to be realistic about your players' abilities and limitations within a given system.

As mentioned, choosing a system and style of play based on the strengths and weaknesses of your players is crucial, at least at this level of play. When we talk about style of play, we are referring to the way a team uses a system by focusing on individual and team strengths. A team using a direct style plays the ball forward as quickly and as directly as possible to get into the attacking third. If you have fast frontrunners and defenders who are sophisticated in serving the long ball, this style of play can be very successful. Various styles of play complement various systems, whereas other styles include, but are not limited to, counterattacking, low-pressure, and possession. Teams often change their styles of play based on upcoming opponents or even combine styles to better complement their athletes.

Many clubs and countries believe in a specific system and style of play and recruit players based on their ability to fit into that particular system and style. At the younger levels, coaches should not force a system of play if their athletes' strengths do not complement that system. Following are a few factors to consider when selecting your system and style of play:

- Your team's strengths and weaknesses, including individual players' physical abilities, technical and tactical levels of play, and psychological makeup
- Your opponent's system and style of play
- Weather and field conditions
- Team feedback after having tested a particular system

The ability of your athletes, the strengths and weaknesses of your opponents, and your own personality all contribute to decisions to modify systems and styles of play. The game often dictates when a team should change a style of play. If you are losing in the final minutes of a game, you don't focus on defense! Hopefully, you make sound adjustments that push players forward and incorporate an attacking style of play in the hope of increasing the score. Although your chosen system is tactically important, ultimately, players, not the systems they are in, win games!

TYPES OF SYSTEMS

Systems of play have come a long way since the early years of soccer when formations focused on high numbers in the attacking third of the field and dribbling was the primary skill. Eventually, soccer developed into a game of teamwork and not just individual talent. As a result, formations became more balanced in the middle and defensive thirds.

Although there are several systems to chose from, every system has variations. You must remain open-minded about which would be best for your team based on the skills of your particular athletes. Following are the four most common systems of play and some of the advantages and disadvantages of each.

The 1-4-4-2 System

The 1-4-4-2 system uses a goalkeeper, four defenders, four midfielders, and two attackers, as shown in figure 14.1, which is the standard alignment for this system. This system is simple to teach because it is fairly balanced; players can easily regain their shape on transition because each side is a mirror image of the other. In other words, the role of the left back is the same as that of the right back.

Variations of the 1-4-4-2 system have the four defenders forming a flat back four formation or using a diamond shape with a sweeper behind the center back or stopper. If your defensive backs are flat and spread out creating width, your midfield can balance that by being in a diamond shape condensing the middle of the field and forcing the opponent to attack up the flank in the space your defensive line can cover

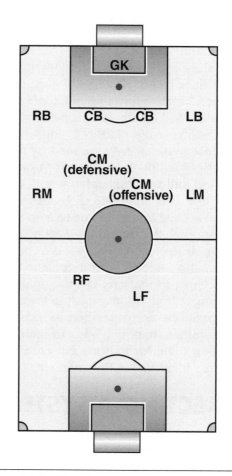

Figure 14.1 Standard alignment for the 1-4-4-2 system.

(see figure 14.2). If your defensive backs are in a diamond shape with a sweeper as shown in figure 14.3, your midfield can play flat and spread out on a line, forcing the opponent to find the gaps between them or play the flanks in the back. As shown in figure 14.1, both the midfield and the defensive backs can play fairly flat as one side mirrors the other and shifts together to stop an attack. Again, the variations you use should depend on your players' abilities and your opponents' tendencies.

In the 1-4-4-2 system, the two attackers typically work closely together and can choose to flood zones with their runs. When attacking, the outside backs should keep their width in the buildup and be prepared to overlap as well as receive balls from the opposite flank for a quick switch. In the attacking half, the majority of the width comes from the outside midfielders, but they also play a role in moving away from the flank to create space for the outside backs looking to overlap. This movement also provides more opportunity for combination play between the two positions.

The central defenders provide critical support during the buildup and can assist in getting their center midfielders to push up and provide support to the two attackers. With the center midfielders pushed up, they can then support the front-runners underneath or make diagonal runs into the opponent's defensive area. Defensively, most teams in this formation have a zonal marking system in the back giving numerical superiority against a two- or three-forward system. This system allows the defense to mark a particularly talented forward; while one player marks, the other three remain in a zone. The two attacking players in this formation have a defensive role in working together to slow the opponent's buildup by pressuring defenders that have won balls or by forcing them to distribute out of a specific side of the field.

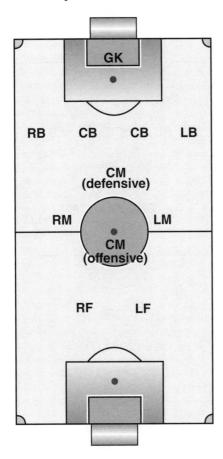

Figure 14.2 Flat back four/diamond mid four alignments for the 1-4-4-2 system.

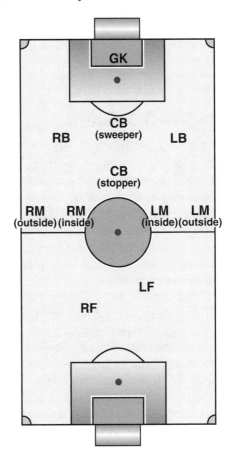

Figure 14.3 Diamond back four/flat mid four alignments for the 1-4-4-2 system.

Advantages

- This system provides a balanced and secure defense.

- This system allows for better shape when regaining possession of the ball.

- Flank midfielders have the option to create width or pinch in and allow the outside back the opportunity to overlap and fill the space.

- The mirror image makes it easy for players to play either side of the field without getting confused about their roles.

Disadvantages

- Putting an extra player in the defense or midfield removes a player from the attack.

- Getting numbers forward in a quick transition on attack can be difficult.

- The opponent can have an opportunity to push a player forward if their three backs can handle your two attackers, especially if your midfielders are not supporting the two front-runners.

The 1-3-4-3 System

The 1-3-4-3 system balances players evenly across the field with a goalkeeper, three defenders, four midfielders, and three attackers. Figure 14.4 shows the standard alignment for this system, which gives teams the ability to attack and defend with seven players. It is considered offensive in character with the three attackers and four midfielders constantly combining for attacking opportunities.

With three attackers, a center forward is used in this system. The midfielders can either provide the width in the defending half or be in a diamond shape. When the midfielders are in a diamond shape, the width is provided by the attacking and defensive players as they spread out toward the sidelines (see figure 14.5). Placing your midfielders in a diamond shape works well if you are playing an opponent who tends to possess and attack up the middle. This shape condenses the middle and forces opponents wide.

Ideally, your two outside forwards use their speed to attack the defense and work closely with the outside midfielders. The center forward often drops to receive passes from her midfielders or defenders. Initially, her job is to hold the ball, drawing a defender while teammates get into good attacking positions. If the defenders position themselves wide, they play a crucial role in helping to switch the ball and change the point of attack.

When the width is generated by the attacking players, it spreads out the opponent's defense, making it easier to attack in the seams. Play can be generated through the midfield or directly to the three front-runners. The outside midfielders and wide attackers need to work well together, as well as with the center forward and the remainder of the midfield.

Defense in the 1-3-4-3 system should begin with pressure from the forwards and tracking the opponent's defense when they are trying to possess the ball out of the back. Midfielders need to track back to create numbers around the ball defensively. The three marking backs

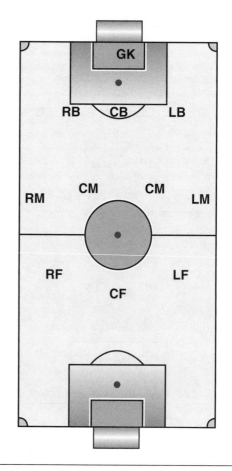

Figure 14.4 Standard alignment for the 1-3-4-3 system.

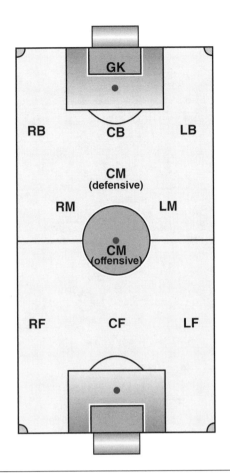

Figure 14.5 Flat back three/diamond mid four alignments for the 1-3-4-3 system.

must have support from a defensive center midfielder and an outside midfielder covering the weak side. Typically, the three backs will play in a zone, but all three need to be willing to have marking responsibilities and have the ability to switch from man-to-man to zone marking until a breakdown in defense is resolved.

The center back must have a good tactical sense of the game and be able to read long-ball service while having confidence in her decision-making abilities. The outside backs should have good speed if possible and know how to provide cover for the other two backs. The three backs must learn to track runs both to the ball and into space.

Players need to learn to track only as long as necessary and then try to regain their shape. They must make split-second decisions about whether it's more important to track a particular run or maintain the space that the ball can be played into. Teaching your athletes how to read the player with the ball will help them de-

termine whether the ball is going to be served to the checking player or into the space that the player has left. Reading the body language of the player with the ball can help your backs recognize "dummy runs" (designed not to receive the ball) and help them to keep their shape in this zonal system. If a defender does track, the center defender must read the pass and cover the space that the tracking defender has left open.

Advantages

- The team has the opportunity to attack consistently with three attackers while still maintaining numbers in the back against an opponent with two attackers.
- Midfield plays with the traditional four and enables the team to play a possession or a direct style of play.
- The team can attack with seven the majority of the time.
- There is more opportunity for double-teaming in the midfield with seven around the ball.
- If you have fast defenders, this system plays to their strength in the outside back position.

Disadvantages

- Attackers must pressure the opponent's defense or they will pay the price with a quick counter or a long diagonal ball served deep into their defensive end.
- Players can be forced to mark in 1v1 situations if playing a team with three attackers.
- Flank midfielders can be forced to track more space to provide necessary balance on the weak side.
- This system could be very difficult if you don't have a tactically strong center defender. All defenders have a greater responsibility to understand when to track runs and read service.

The 1-3-5-2 System

The 1-3-5-2 system uses a goalkeeper, three defenders, five midfielders, and two attackers, as shown in figure 14.6, which is the standard

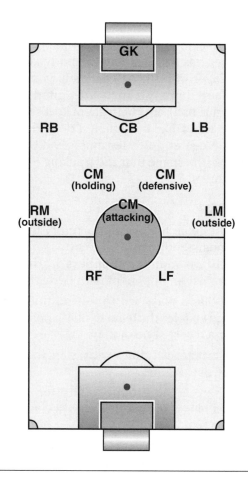

Figure 14.6 Standard alignment for the 1-3-5-2 system.

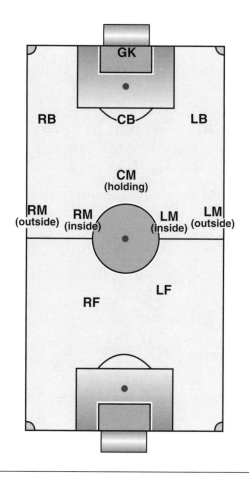

Figure 14.7 Variation in midfield alignment for the 1-3-5-2 system.

alignment for this system. Figure 14.7 shows a variation in the midfield alignment that can be used effectively based on your players' abilities and your opponents' tendencies. The 1-3-5-2 system is very popular with older and professional teams. With increased numbers in the midfield, the team can control the middle of the field. This creates greater numbers in the attack because the five midfielders can easily join the two forwards for greater attacking opportunities.

The three defenders can form a flat back three formation or use two defenders to mark the attackers while the third defender takes on a sweeper role. In a three back zone, cover is handled by balancing the weak-side defender. The location of the ball and the amount of pressure on the ball determine how much the weak-side defender balances. The closer to the penalty box the opponent with the ball is, the less balance is required. If there is too much bal-

ance, the opponent will have room to penetrate. Correct positioning of the weak-side defender also allows her to track runs behind the center back. The goalkeeper must communicate the positioning of the weak-side defender. At the same time, the goalkeeper plays a vital role in dominating the space behind the zone and winning deep through balls. The outside midfielders are also key in balancing the weak side, but even more so if the defense has two backs responsible for marking and a sweeper.

The five midfielders can organize themselves by placing two midfielders wide and three central midfielders in a diamond shape, or they can spread out in a curved line. Having five in the midfield can also give your team the advantage of using one player to focus on marking a particularly threatening midfielder on the opposing team, while still leaving you with four zoning midfielders. On the attack, the outside midfielders provide width and allow a more indirect or possession style of play because of the numerical advantage with three supporting center midfielders. The two attackers remain up top with one positioned as a center striker and the other a floating striker. These two attackers can exchange roles, or both can float and work together for attacking combinations as in a 1-4-4-2. However, in this formation they should have more support from their midfielders, while getting a minimum of six players in the attack.

When building the attack out of the back, the two outside backs should stay wide. The weak-side back will drop slightly to keep her shape and prepare for the switch. The outside backs should focus on attacking up the flank and draw the opponent into shifting to that side. Combination play with the midfielders and attackers making diagonal runs should provide the backs with several options for an organized attack. Again, with any three-back system, the center back must read the game well and communicate successfully with her outside backs and goalkeeper. She must have the confidence to track the space behind her outside backs and the ability to stay calm and organized when a breakdown in the defense occurs.

Advantages

- Five midfielders allow for better possession in that zone while giving numeric advantage when playing an opponent with a four-player midfield system.

- The two attackers typically get better support from the attacking midfielders.

- Both the offense and defense have greater support and the opportunity to double-team with more players supporting off the ball.

Disadvantages

- An organized offense can spread the defense thin and exploit the space.

- Defense has more space to cover and more responsibilities; it can struggle against an opponent's three front if support is not sufficient from the midfield.

- This system can be difficult in the back when playing an opponent that is direct and good at hitting the long diagonal ball and exploiting the space over the top.

The 1-4-3-3 System

The 1-4-3-3 system uses a goalkeeper, four defenders, three midfielders, and three attackers, as shown in figure 14.8, which is the standard alignment for this system. Figure 14.9 shows a variation of the standard 1-4-3-3 alignment by placing the midfielders in a flat formation. The 1-4-3-3 has become increasingly popular in today's game because it offers good offensive opportunities, and it can quickly turn into a very defensive and compact 1-4-5-1 formation. This system provides the numbers in the back that can handle an opponent playing with a three-player front.

The defenders can form a flat back four formation or use a sweeper positioned behind the other three backs. The midfielders should stay pinched in, forming a triangular shape with one center midfielder behind the two attacking center midfielders (or their positions can be

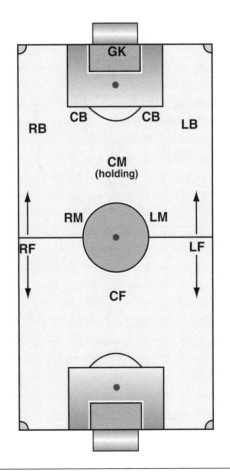

Figure 14.8 Standard alignment for the 1-4-3-3 system.

reversed with two dropped and one high). Using a triangle shape in the middle helps control the center of the field and forces the opponent to play the ball wide rather than attacking straight up the middle.

The midfield can also spread out in a line and play flat, as shown in figure 14.9. Playing linearly can leave big gaps in the midfield because the midfielders are spread out rather than condensed, as they are in the triangle shape. This makes it more difficult to stop penetration up the middle of the field, particularly when playing against an opponent with four midfielders. However, dropping two outside forwards can help solve this problem. You would only want to do this when you are trying to secure a lead and the opposition is sending several players forward in the closing minutes to try to even the score.

Dropping the two forwards and shaping the midfield in a curved or arched line gives your team a very compact 1-4-5-1 and easily

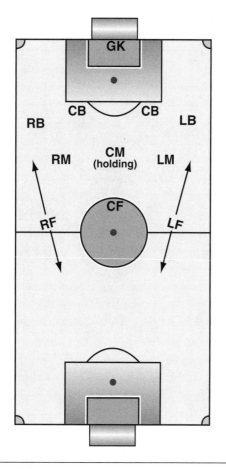

Figure 14.9 Variation in midfield alignment for the 1-4-3-3 system.

condenses the space, making it difficult for the opponent to penetrate. Keep in mind that attacking opportunities for your team are limited at that point because you have only one player forward. If this player is good at holding on to the ball, you would want your players to play a ball to her feet and allow the supporting runs to come from the two dropped forwards and supporting midfielders.

The attackers spread out and create width up top, which spreads out the opponent's defense. It is important for the attackers to pressure the defense and not allow them to serve long balls. They are also responsible for pressuring back and helping their midfielders double-team on the flanks. This system is very much an attacking system; the ball is played quickly to the attacking players with a long-ball service from the back line players.

The midfielders support the attackers and defenders. Long balls served should go over the top and into the space behind the defense, as well as to the feet of a checking attacker. Varying the service will not only help keep the opponent's defense guessing, but also keep them off balance. The attackers should concentrate on closing the flanks and not allow the opponent's marking backs to counter up the sideline because the flank midfield is usually the weakness in this system. By forcing the opponent's backs to go up the middle rather than wide, attackers and midfielders have a better chance of regaining possession.

The defense in this system will play in a zone with two center defenders working closely together (with one sweeping as an option). Because the midfielders are usually outnumbered in this system, teams will try to exploit this area. The midfielders will find they have a lot of ground to cover, especially against a team that possesses well up the middle. To help the midfielders, the outside backs must cover the flanks and overlap when the opportunity presents itself.

Advantages

- This system allows for greater numbers in the attack.
- Four players remain in the back for defensive stability, making it harder for the opponent to find the space to penetrate.

- The opponent's defense experiences high pressure with three chasing attackers.
- This system makes it easier to possess the ball in the back and establish a buildup in the attack, especially against an opponent playing with two attackers.
- The defense has an easier time running the offside trap.

Disadvantages

- The team is outnumbered in the midfield against most systems.
- If the three attackers don't provide pressure against the opponent's defense, the team could be vulnerable with numbers down in a quick counterattack.
- One good-quality serve from the opponent's backs to their midfield could leave the team defending with numbers down.

Part V

COACHING GAMES

CHAPTER 15 PREPARING FOR A GAME

Preparation for a game involves more than just making sure your team is physically prepared to perform. Being adequately prepared for game day requires that you also scout the opponent and spend time in practice focusing on the situations your team is likely to face with that opponent. Your girls should also be mentally prepared for the challenges game day can bring. Pregame and halftime routines, prepared ahead of time and adhered to consistently, will also help the team on game day. Finally, an important pregame task is choosing the starting lineup.

SCOUTING THE OPPONENT

Scouting the opponent provides specific information your team can use when preparing for a game. As a coach, you will need to take the time to attend other teams' games. If you are unable to do so because of your schedule, send a reliable assistant in your place, or send another person to videotape the opponent. If you are not able to personally scout an opponent or send someone in your place, you can still gather basic information about the team by reading newspaper articles about past games or networking with other coaches who have played your opponent.

It is best to scout an opponent within two weeks of playing them to get a true sense of their strengths and weaknesses. Watching teams two months before playing them will not help because teams evolve, injuries change lineups, and athletes change positions.

When scouting an opponent, keep the big picture in mind. In addition to watching individual players and their positions on the field, pay attention to the tendencies of the coaching staff in regard to strategies and plays. Following are some questions you will want to answer about an opponent:

- What type of system, or formation, do they play?
- What is their style of play?
- Do they play direct or indirect, or a combination of both?
- What are their set plays like, and who typically takes them?
- Do they attack a certain side or look to serve a particular player?
- Do they target specific players on corner kicks?
- Do they have players who are dangerous in the attacking third with long throws? What is their shape in the back?

- Are they flat, or do they play with a sweeper?

- Are they strong in the air?

- Do they zone or man-mark, or a combination of both?

- What are their midfield tendencies?

- Do they hold and dribble, or distribute quickly?

- Do they like to receive the ball at their feet or run on to it in space?

- What are the strengths and weaknesses of the goalkeeper?

- Do they distribute well?

- Do they have a tendency to play off the line?

- Do they have a big presence in goal?

As you watch the team you are scouting in action, you will want to keep track of the information you gather. You can use a preexisting scouting form, as shown in figure 15.1, which usually provides space for all the information you need; you can just fill in the blanks while focusing on the game. Most observation, or analysis, forms include sections on system of play, style of play, attacking and defensive shape and tendencies, set plays, key players, goalkeeper's style of play, and overall team strengths and weaknesses.

You may find you work more efficiently by writing freely while scouting rather than using a form. One way to do this is to keep a binder of all of your opponents each season and take notes each time you scout. You can also log game results for future reference in case you play a team again later in the season. After scouting a specific opponent, you will want to transfer important notes onto a preexisting scouting form so you can organize the information you need to highlight and review with your team.

Keep in mind that scouting can be misused and give athletes a false sense of what is going to happen in a game. Your athletes must understand that the information gathered from scouting is used to help develop a game plan, but that during a game, anything can happen. Remind them that the information you have is based on competition with a different team on a different day and that their focus should always remain on their own efforts and how they will prepare to win, not solely on their opponent's efforts.

TRAINING FOR THE GAME

Preparing for a game against a specific opponent begins in the practice sessions prior to the game. You will need to prepare your athletes so that they have the utmost confidence heading into the game. They will need the proper balance of technical and tactical sessions and mental training, as well as proper rest, recovery, and nutrition. This is not an easy balance to achieve. Most important is that you remain flexible and pay close attention to how your athletes are feeling, particularly on the day before a game.

PREGAME PRACTICES

One or two practices prior to a game, you will want to discuss and practice the types of situations your players are going to face with the upcoming opponent. However, do not focus completely on the opponent's strengths and weaknesses. Review concerns and tendencies of the opponent's top players, but then walk through your own attack and discuss how you can break down the opposing defense, emphasizing your own team strengths. Focusing too much on the opponent can result in your athletes' focusing on the things they cannot necessarily control.

If you know your opponent, either through scouting, as discussed previously, or because you've already played them during the season, then you'll have specific topics and situations to review in practice. Although the focus of most practice sessions is to develop your players individually, strengthen the weaknesses of the team, and continue to acknowledge what they are already doing well, as game day approaches, part of your focus now shifts to preparing for your opponent by minimizing the team's strengths and exploiting its weaknesses.

Help raise the confidence level of your team by putting your players in situations they will face in the upcoming game. For example, if you know the opponent plays very direct with a lot of speed up front, emphasize putting your defense under constant pressure with long balls and having fast forwards run at them. One way to do this is to have some of the players from a boys' team, or male assistant coaches, step in and play the role of the fast forwards. This type

Opponent Scouting Report

Team: _____ versus _____

Final score: _____

<table>
<tr><td>**System of Play**</td><td></td><td>**Style of Play**</td></tr>
</table>

Defenders

Flat or sweep:

Zone or man-to-man:

Gaps (big or small):

Set plays:

Midfielders

Flat or diamond:

Central or through the wings:

Playmaker:

Set plays:

Forwards

Staggered or flat:

Penetrating runs:

Checking runs:

Take-on or layoff:

Set plays:

Goalkeepers

Strengths:

Weaknesses:

<table>
<tr><td>**Scorers**</td><td></td><td>**Individual Standout Players**</td></tr>
</table>

General Impressions:

From *Coaching Girls' Soccer Successfully* by Debra LaPrath, 2009, Champaign, IL: Human Kinetics.

Figure 15.1

of training is especially helpful in a big game that you know will be a battle from beginning to end. Any edge you can give your team will be beneficial.

Again, do not spend entire practice sessions focusing on the opponent's strengths and weaknesses. It is critical that you focus on your own team's strengths to reinforce the things your girls are doing well. You must also work to minimize their weaknesses by making adjustments either in your lineup, your strategy, or your system. If it is early in the season, don't be afraid to revisit your system if things are not going as planned. On the other hand, don't make constant adjustments every time the girls make mistakes. Give them the space and opportunity to learn from their mistakes before you decide that changes are necessary. The following is a list of specific topics to review at practice prior to a game.

- *Attacking and defensive shape.* Make sure your girls understand their attacking and defensive responsibilities. This will help them avoid confusion when the opponent attempts to disrupt their strategy. In addition, if you are trying to secure a lead in the closing minutes and your team is in an attacking system with three forwards, the athletes know that the captains (with your approval) can drop a player into the defensive line to secure the back.

- *Team strategy for the game.* Because you don't play every team the same way, your athletes must have a strategy for each game. For example, if your opponent is particularly strong in the middle of the field, most likely your strategy will be to attack up the flank when possible.

- *Set plays.* Your set plays must be rehearsed frequently so your athletes know which play to use in a given situation. They must know who is doing what so the setup is instantaneous without your direction. Spend time at every practice on set plays; they are game changing and a lot of fun when players are confident in their responsibilities. Make sure you execute set plays in gamelike scenarios in which the pressure is on the player.

- *Penalty kicks.* Your team must know the top five kickers without a doubt. There should be no question about who should take a penalty kick

if the situation arises. Players should not need to look to you for approval. They should know because they have reviewed it every day in practice. Allow your top five to ten penalty kick takers to hit their shots with the added pressure of the walk from midfield and silence from the team while waiting for the referee's whistle.

Jared's Wig

One season we were preparing for a quarterfinal game in our sectional play-offs. Our opponent had who they thought was the top striker in the county. She was fast and had already been given credit for most goals scored a season at her school. Their game plan was to get her the ball and let the magic happen. But we had plans of our own. Fortunately for us, we had speed in our defensive line, and her nickname was Doctor. Doctor could chase anybody down, but we wanted more from her that night; we wanted her to beat that forward to the ball every time!

All week in training, our fast assistant coach, Jared, put on a wig and pretended to be the opponent's forward. He ran at Doctor all week long, and they battled for balls. By the end of the week, she was either beating him to the ball or knocking him down. It was an awesome sight and made us constantly laugh at practice. That lightheartedness was really helpful in keeping the team from getting uptight and taking things too seriously in the play-off preparation.

Needless to say, after dealing with Jared's speed all week, Doctor was ready for the opponent and shut her down all night. When the opponent's defense would send the long ball to their star forward, their home crowd would instantly stand and make noise in anticipation of a great goal. Well, that goal never happened. I'm not sure how many times she touched the ball (very few to my recollection), but I do know that Doctor beat her to the ball every time in dedication to Jared and his wig!

Mental Preparation

The game is the ultimate test of an athlete's ability, character, and mental toughness. For some athletes, the pressure to perform well can be overwhelming. In these situations, a player must rely on both physical and mental habits. Players have different mental routines when preparing for a game, but the result should be the same: an ideal competitive state. Mental skills, like physical skills, can be learned and developed with practice, as discussed in chapter 6. Quite often, the thing that holds an athlete back from having a satisfying performance is not her skill or knowledge of the game, but rather the psychological barriers she puts on herself.

The ultimate goal of your athletes' mental preparation is to reach their individual performance potentials. That potential cannot be reached if they are unable to focus in training. One of the biggest frustrations for a coach is when the team lacks mental focus in the training session prior to playing an opponent the athletes know will not be much of a challenge. However, if you've spent time developing quality leadership in your captains and veteran players, they will help you demand the necessary focus and set the tone for the younger or less mature players.

You can do many things to create a focused environment for your players. When players work hard technically and physically, they gain confidence and the mental toughness that comes from solid preparation. Through hard work, self discipline, and teamwork, players learn to stay mentally positive despite setbacks.

In addition to preparing your players technically and physically, you can also help them achieve relaxation and focus prior to a game. You may find it helpful to have them write out visualizations or imagery. When used properly, visualizations can be an important part of your players' pregame preparation. As discussed in chapter 3, detailed visualizations of successful situations, such as scoring a goal or making a save, improve performance.

Prior to each game, you may also have your players fill out and sign a commitment contract (see figure 15.2), which emphasizes performance and controlling the things they can control. These contracts hold players accountable for their actions. When they verbally tell their teammates they will commit to something, they have 21 other girls expecting them to keep their word. Players' commitments should be realistic and positive. These commitments can change from game to game depending on the circumstances or the opponent. At the practice prior to a game, close with each player sharing her commitment with the rest of the team.

DETERMINING GAME ROUTINES

Solidifying your team's pregame routines is important for both the coaching staff and the players. Knowing what's expected before a game helps to alleviate any unnecessary pregame anxiety. Players like to have routines, and most are adamant about sticking to them. You will, of course, set specific guidelines, such as arrival time and equipment responsibilities. Your players, however, may have other routines that they pass on to one another from season to season. On our team, all the athletes touch the upper corner of the goalpost as they run by. We don't ask why!

Game Arrival

Specific game routines are important so that players and staff get right to the business of focusing on the game. Lack of routine leaves players aimless, unfocused, and unprepared. For example, when arriving at a facility—for both home and away games—our team does not go onto the field until each player is present and accounted for, so that we can walk in together. This simple gesture accomplishes two things: First, it shows that every player is important enough to wait for (unless we know they are going to be late for a particular reason), and second, it portrays that we are there together as a team and will play together regardless of the circumstances. Typically, the team waits by the front entrance or in the locker room. When everyone is ready, they walk across the field together toward the bench. Once they reach the bench, they lay out their bags and gear and begin their warm-up.

Pregame Warm-Up

Before every game, your players must warm up. A proper warm-up not only gets them physically prepared for the game, but also focuses them on the task before them. Players should have a say in their warm-up; after all, the warm-up is for them, not the coaching staff. However, any changes in a warm-up should be discussed and rehearsed in practice prior to the game.

Your pregame warm-up should be dynamic, meaning that it should include specific activities

Commitment Contract

I, _____, pledge with all my heart to participate in the game on _____ against _____ as a significant contributor to the team by displaying desire, commitment, persistence, courage, and confidence that will result in a successful competition and a successful season. To show how serious I am, I commit to:

1.

2.

3.

I accept my role on this team and will fulfill it as I have specified in this contract.

Player's signature:_____

Date: _____

From *Coaching Girls' Soccer Successfully* by Debra LaPrath, 2009, Champaign, IL: Human Kinetics.

Figure 15.2

Clearly communicating the importance of a focused and productive pregame warm-up to your athletes should be a priority.

for the various positions. For example, have your midfielders play one- and two-touch small-sided games that include gamelike movements and activities (see figure 15.3).

The warm-up should also include time for the players to stretch on their own. Allowing them to stretch or visualize on their own, if time permits, is a great way to show that you respect their individual game preparation routines. They will be grateful for your trust and the freedom you give them to do what they need to do!

The total warm-up can be anywhere from 35 to 50 minutes long depending on the time available based on travel or field set-up times. If time is short, adjustments should be made accordingly. You cannot always predict traffic, carpool, or equipment delays. If you have to make adjustments to your warm-up, try to include all segments, but take a few minutes off each one. You can prepare your team for the inevitable shortened warm-up by practicing it before the game and giving the players a say in what areas to leave out if necessary.

The pregame warm-up can tell you a lot about your players' readiness to perform. It can tell you whether they are focused or easily distracted, if they are loose or uptight. As you watch your team warm up, you can check in with athletes individually to see how they are doing.

Halftime

Unlike many other sports, once a soccer game begins, halftime is the only opportunity you have to address the entire team before the end of the game, so you must be prepared. After 40 minutes of physical and mental focus, the girls get 10 minutes to recharge before they have to go out there and give all they have for another 40 minutes. During halftime, first allow your players a minute or so to get a drink and talk with each other before you start talking to them about the game. If possible, walk the team away from the field so they aren't distracted by fans, family, or friends. Following are some things to accomplish during halftime:

• Allow your captains and veteran players to start the dialogue, if they want or need to. They are captains because they have earned the respect of the team. Their focus should be team strategy, areas for improvement, and what seems to be working well. If they wander into other areas, redirect them in a subtle way and then discuss their approach later, one on one.

• Discuss necessary adjustments, limiting your instruction to no more than three key points. Discussing too many things at once is likely to put your athletes on overload, and ultimately, they will tune you out, particularly if

Sample Pregame Warm-Up

3-4 min.	Warm-up run	Mental and physical warm-up; getting focused
6-8 min.	Stretching	Muscle warm-up/flexibility
6-10 min.	Tempo runs, sprints, final stretch	Sprints, change of pace
5-7 min.	Circle drill	Passing and receiving
8-10 min.	Crossing and finishing drill	Shooting, timing, headers, crossing
3-4 min.	Long balls for the defense	Positional activity for service
5-6 min.	Corners (offense and defense)	Offensive and defensive organization
5 min.	Scrimmage	Game readiness, support, passing angles
3-4 min.	Coin toss (captains)	Determines possession and field side
2 min.	Sprint circle and team cheer	Getting fired up; team unity

Figure 15.3

they are down at the half. They will be fatigued and will need this time to rejuvenate mentally and physically. Too much information can add to their stress and anxiety. Halftime is the time to recharge, so be very specific about what you want from them in the next 40 minutes.

• Address the positive aspects of the first half. You may sometimes believe there isn't anything positive to address. Nevertheless, without sugarcoating the game, dig deep and find a few things that are worth mentioning.

• Check in with players who may have injuries or who have had a very physical first half. Make sure that they are capable of playing at 100 percent capacity. Let them know you are aware that something is wrong and that they need to communicate the problem with you. Remind them that they are not doing themselves or their teammates any favors by playing injured. By being proactive and paying attention to your athletes, you can help avoid more serious injuries later.

DETERMINING THE STARTING LINEUP

When choosing your starting lineup, consider athletes' work rates and effectiveness in training (working hard and working smart), their performances in previous games, the chemistry of the lineup, the opponent and player match-ups, injuries or illnesses, discipline problems, and players' attitudes. Soccer is a team sport, and most of these factors affect the team in one way or another.

A classic starting lineup scenario is allowing a top athlete to start when she has been a discipline problem or has taken on a negative tone or attitude with the coach or her teammates. By continuing to play the athlete, the coach sends a strong message to the team that rules and behavior standards apply only to certain players. As a result, the coach has a bigger problem to deal with: a team that doesn't trust her words or her actions.

Some coaches do not announce the final lineup until after the pregame warm-up just prior to kickoff. However, some coaches believe that their athletes need more time to process whether they are starting or not, so they announce their starters at the practice before the game. I prefer to wait until game day to announce my starters because in my experience this has been an effective way of getting the best warm-up out of each athlete. An inspired warm-up from a nonstarter or an athlete who may typically split playing time has changed our starting lineup on several occasions and has served as a wake-up call for a starter who is taking her pregame preparation for granted!

A few times during the season, I give each of my athletes a copy of a field and ask them to fill in the best starting lineup for the next game. These lineups are submitted anonymously for the coaching staff to review prior to the game. Allowing your players to have input gives them an opportunity to express their desires and be heard.

CHAPTER 16 HANDLING GAME-DAY SITUATIONS

Nothing is more exciting than the day of the game, especially when you are playing one of your top rivals. With all the excitement and enthusiasm for the competition, you'll need to remain focused on the task before you while making sure your players as well as your coaching staff are prepared for situations that will arise before, during, and after the game.

BEFORE THE GAME

You will have many things to take care of before the game, including arranging transportation, setting the team's arrival time at the field, and considering your starting lineup. Two important tasks you should not overlook are pregame nutrition and motivating your players for the competition.

Pregame Nutrition

Teach your athletes to fuel their bodies properly before games so they have the energy to perform at their best. Many young student-athletes have developed poor eating habits that are difficult to change. You can do several things to encourage healthy eating habits, starting at your preseason parent meeting. Remind parents of the importance of working together

to help the girls make good nutrition choices. Encourage your athletes to pay attention to how they feel when they've eaten well, and educate them by relating nutrition to performance and recovery. Remind them that all their work, both mental and physical, will have optimal results only if they are persistent in maintaining good nutrition and hydration habits.

Make a commitment to pay attention to the energy levels of all your athletes, but particularly those who seem to exhaust quickly at practices and games. Encourage those needing special attention to keep a food log in which they record how they feel and what their energy levels are. Have them check in with you every couple of days so you can discuss the log and decide if they need to make any changes. If their nutrition habits seem to be extreme and affecting their performance and weight, meet with their parents and recommend a nutritionist.

Pregame Motivation

Each player has her own way of getting motivated for a game, including individual pregame routines that help clear her mind and prepare her for performing. Give your girls their time in the locker room to do what they need to do to motivate themselves. Some may need to listen to music, others may need quiet, whereas others may be loud and talkative.

In addition to their individual motivating rituals, the team should have some rituals they share. At our home games, the girls walk down the path to our stadium and wait at the gate until I start playing the pregame music; then they step out as a team. On game days, the girls on the team eat lunch together and wear the same practice shirts or sweats.

DURING THE GAME

The coaching staff has many responsibilities during the game. Two important things to pay attention to and be prepared for are the need to adjust the game plan when things don't go as planned, as well as coach and player conduct.

Adjusting the Game Plan

As your team plays, take time (or appoint an assistant coach or other person) to analyze the game so that you are prepared to make adjustments to your game plan at halftime, if necessary.

Pay attention to the entire field, not just the ball, and make notes regarding both your team and the opponent. Following are the types of things you should be on the lookout for to help you make the most appropriate adjustments:

Your Team's Defense

- What is the overall shape of your defense (pressure, cover, balance)?
- Are your players marking goal-side?
- Are your players making good decisions after winning the ball?
- Are your players communicating and preventing shots?

Your Team's Offense

- What is the overall shape of your offense?
- Are your players making correct runs with proper timing?
- Are your players creating and taking shots?

- Are your players possessing?
- Are your midfielders spreading the field and changing the point of attack?

The Opponent's Defense

- What is the overall shape of the opponent's defense?
- Does the opponent look for man-to-man matchups that you can exploit?
- Are there gaps in the opponent's defense, and if so, where are they?
- What are the opponent goalkeeper's strengths and weaknesses?

The Opponent's Offense

- What is the overall shape of the opponent's offense?
- Does the opponent target a specific player?
- Is the opponent scoring, and if so, how?
- What are the opponent's set plays, and is there a specific threat (e.g., a long throw)?

The more games you watch, the easier it becomes to analyze the field. Breaking the game down in this way will help you make halftime adjustments or know what specific topics to address in training. Keep in mind, however, the importance of teaching your players to solve problems on their own. Make it a point to cover gamelike situations that mirror the intensity and pressure players will encounter during actual games in practice so your players know they are capable of making decisions on their own during competition with opponents.

If you are in the lead and the clock is winding down, remind players to be conservative in their runs without a blatant delay of game. If you are down, your players should be prepared to adjust the lineup when you need to send extra players forward in the attack. If rehearsed, these changes should give your team a boost of confidence rather than cause anxiety. Soccer players need to be students of the game and develop the ability to read the movement and flow of the game while making split-second decisions without hesitation. The more you allow your athletes to make decisions on their own, the more they will trust their own intuition.

Doctor's Breakthrough

Doctor worked hard on and off the field and committed herself 100 percent in everything she did. She was a fierce competitor and absolutely hated to lose!

Following is an excerpt from a letter Doctor wrote to me a few years after she graduated. In it she describes a situation in which she overcame the fear of failure and found the courage to trust her own voice. Sometimes, as hard as it may be, you have to let a player learn how to come through on her own.

"I have so many excellent memories from my sophomore to senior years, but one that keeps playing in my mind comes from a league game in my junior year. I was playing defense, and I felt like I had absolutely no support from the other defenders. Our goalkeeper was having one of "those games," and we were getting pounded, ball after ball. I felt that all the hard work I was doing was useless. I remember running over to the sideline, fighting back heavy tears, and asking you what to do. I know you could see I was ready to break, but you told me at that point that I had to make a decision whether to keep fighting or get pulled. You weren't going to tell me what to do. I looked in your eyes, and I looked deep down within myself and decided to push through. It was crazy—my whole attitude changed, my energy went back up, and I fought even harder till the game ended. It was nothing you forced me to do, but you helped me reach SO far down into my character (farther than I ever had before) and dig out something I thought I didn't have. Thank you for that. That moment has served me in my life far beyond the soccer field."

Coach and Player Conduct

Although you expect your players to behave in a positive and respectful manner regardless of the situation, incidents will arise that will test your patience and composure. If you are clear and adamant about your philosophy and behavior expectations, you will find that the problems that come up will become benchmarks for the rest of the team.

Generally, an athlete who has lost her composure will feel remorse about her behavior, especially if it has affected the team in a negative way. This is an especially important teaching moment you should not let pass. As soon as possible, discuss with the athlete ways she can control her behavior when she becomes angry or upset about a situation. Most athletes want clear boundaries and are willing to conform when they know they will be held accountable for their actions.

Sometimes emotions get the best of us when we believe a decision isn't right after having invested so much time and energy in a game. Controlling your emotions when officials make errors or seem to be favoring the other team is one of the many challenges you will face throughout your coaching career. Staying calm can be difficult when you and your team have worked hard and you believe you aren't getting fair calls. Constantly commenting or yelling disapproving remarks will not get you the results you want. If anything, you'll continue to get unfavorable calls. Your behavior can also provoke the crowd into getting involved, which does no one any good.

Your attitude toward the officials will be reflected in your team's behavior. Your players need to see you greeting and conversing with the officials prior to the game. If the fairness of an official's performance is questionable, you can write a letter or call and voice your concerns to your league commissioner or head official. During the game, however, even if you believe an official is not being fair and making mistakes that are detrimental to your team, you must still maintain a respectful relationship. Officials make our games possible and legitimate, and we cannot compete without them.

Just as you must display good sporting behavior with the officials, so must your athletes with their opponents. Soccer is a contact sport. Accidents and injuries will happen as a result of that contact, and you must talk with your athletes about their behavior when this happens. If an athlete from the other team seems to be purposely going after players rather than the ball, make the officials aware of your concerns. Physical play and questionable calls will be a part of the game, and like anything else in life, it's not what happens but how you react to the situation that matters most. Seeing your players disappointed with the results of a game is difficult, but this is the most important time to emphasize good sporting behavior. If your athletes have learned how to focus on their performance and not just the result, then accepting defeat and congratulating the opponent should not be difficult. You cannot control your players' emotions while they are playing in the game, but you can pull them out of the game for unacceptable behavior.

AFTER THE GAME

You need to have a system in place for the things that must happen after a game, such as the postgame handshake, cool-down, and meeting.

Postgame Handshake

The first thing your players should do after the game is give a quick cheer for the opponents and then walk to the middle of the field to shake their hands and tell them "good game." Some of the girls may know players on the other team either socially or from playing together on club teams. The handshake gives them the opportunity to check in, congratulate one another, and make sure there are no hard feelings after the competition. The girls who do not know anyone on the other team can use this time to give them high fives and exhibit good sporting behavior. Your players should then proceed to the officials and shake their hands and thank them for officiating the game.

Postgame Cool-Down

After the game, your athletes should cool down for approximately 10 to 15 minutes with light jogging, stride walks, and stretching. The benefits of a cool-down are numerous. The most important is the removal of lactic acid buildup in the muscles, which speeds recovery and helps to reduce muscle soreness the next day. Your athletes will usually be sore the day after competition, but a proper cool-down can help to reduce that soreness. Your cool-down routine can use many of the same aerobic movements, runs, and stretching exercises as the pregame warm-up, as shown in figure 16.1.

Postgame Meeting

After the game, when your players have properly cooled down, gather them for a brief postgame meeting to discuss the game. During this meeting, highlight the things the players did well as a

Regardless of the outcome of a game, congratulating and acknowledging your opponents in a positive way are important displays of good sporting behavior.

Sample Postgame Cool-Down

3 min.	Sideline runs (slow jog)	Helps remove lactic acid buildup, decreases heart rate
2 min.	Long stride steps (lunges)	Lengthens muscles
3 min.	Shuffles, side steps	Slow movement helps loosen tight muscles
5 min.	Individual and partner stretching	Helps reduce muscle soreness, improves range of motion
2 min.	Players' choice	Any stretch or movement players personally need or like

Figure 16.1

team, in addition to giving praise to outstanding individual performances. Obviously, a win or loss can affect the overall tone of the postgame meeting, but the emphasis should always be on how the team played.

Losing can be tough on your players when they've worked hard. It is important in these moments to help them keep the game in perspective and outline what they can take away from the loss that will help them become a better team. After the discussion, you can gather into a tight circle and do a postgame cheer. At that time, remind players of their equipment and cleanup duties and check the stat book to confirm goals and assists for the newspaper, if necessary. If a newspaper has sent a reporter, you and some of your athletes may spend a few minutes answering questions and discussing the game.

Consider practicing the 24-hour rule: Give your players no more than 24 hours to celebrate a win or sulk over a loss. Analyze the game enough to make necessary corrections or use it to guide you in the choices you make for your next training sessions, but do not dwell on it or overevaluate its meaning. Remember, your team is only as good as its last practice!

Part VI

COACHING EVALUATION

CHAPTER 17 EVALUATING YOUR PLAYERS

To have a successful soccer program and to be the best coach you can be, you must be willing to put in the time and energy to evaluate your athletes. Without honest evaluations, players can take on a false sense of their own abilities, accomplishments, and contributions to the team and, as a result, never learn to take constructive criticism. Most athletes at this level have been evaluated many times in their athletic careers and understand its importance. When evaluating players, strive to find the balance between complimenting them and pointing out areas in need of improvement.

Opportunities to evaluate your athletes occur both in the preseason and during the season. In the preseason, opportunities occur during camps, tryouts, and player–coach meetings. During the season, you can evaluate your players during practices, when determining your lineup, during games, and after games.

PRESEASON EVALUATIONS

Depending on your league and state policies, as well as your level of play, preseason evaluation opportunities may occur at camps, tryouts, and any player–coach meetings you schedule right before the season begins.

Camps

Prior to tryouts, our high school soccer team holds a summer camp that is open to students from local schools. It is used as a fund-raiser for our program. Although summer camps are not mandatory, we recommend that our players attend as many as they can. Typically, players in their junior and senior years attend camps at the colleges they are interested in attending.

The camp offered at our school is run the week before tryouts and is highly recommended for several reasons. First, it gives the players and coaches the opportunity to get to know one another in a relaxed atmosphere without the pressure of tryouts. It gives the younger or new athletes a look at their competition and usually a better understanding of their skill level compared to the other athletes trying out. This can help them decide whether to try out for the junior varsity or varsity team. Finally, the camp gives the veteran and returning players a chance to check in with each other and reconnect prior to tryouts, which require a lot of intensity and focus.

As you know, emotions can run high during tryouts when athletes are tense from the pressure of trying to make the team. At our school we stress that the camp is *not* a tryout. It incorporates both technical and tactical skills training and competitive small-sided games. And then there are the competitions of the day! The returning players look forward to these because the competition gets fierce. Winning these friendly but intense challenges becomes a matter of pride. It is always a pleasure to see younger players beat out veterans during these competitions; they always get excited, and there is never any animosity from the older players. Actually, it can be quite the opposite: The veteran players recognize that these new players may have an immediate impact on the team, and they are very excited about that.

Our camp generally consists of three-hour sessions Monday through Thursday the week before tryouts. The emphasis is on enjoying the competition and scrimmages. Veteran players have an opportunity to play with and get back in touch with their old teammates and get a feel for the new ones. Camp is especially helpful for the new and younger players who are anxious about tryouts. Because the emphasis is having fun, the new players get a chance to experience the coaches and veteran players on a more personal level. We see to it that the athletes choose a variety of partners throughout the week rather than gravitate only to the teammates they know. By the end of the week, team chemistry is already forming between veteran and new players, just in time for the following week's tryouts!

Tryouts

Different coaches have different ideas on how tryouts should be run. The number of days available for tryouts and how much time you have before your first game will obviously influence how you organize your tryouts. In general, during tryouts you are looking for players' fitness levels, technical skill levels, and tactical and decision-making abilities. You are also looking at their leadership qualities and personalities and the chemistry they have with other athletes. In addition, when you have your first tryout session and know who is trying out for the team, you should look at their grades to get an indication of their work ethic in the classroom.

Assuming you have three days for tryouts, begin on day 1 with an introduction by the coaching staff. Let the athletes know what you are looking for in terms of fitness and skill level

as well as personal qualities and characteristics. Let them know from the beginning that they will not be able to hide on your team, that their personalities and character traits will be revealed. Explain that you expect them to have fun and enjoy the competition, but that they must be prepared for practices that are long and hard. They will be required to invest a lot in the team, both physically and emotionally.

On the first day of tryouts, take notes and stay in constant communication with the other coaches regarding players' strengths and weaknesses. After that first day, you and your fellow coaches should determine (without letting the players know) which returning athletes are a definite yes so that you can focus on new players and returning players who may be struggling to make the team this time around.

Depending on the number of players who graduated out of your program the previous season, you may be looking to fill only a few positions. On the other hand, you may have many positions to fill. However, you're always looking for the talented athlete who can play any position while remaining a focused team player.

You may have some girls at tryouts who work really hard, but just do not have the skills to make the team. These are often girls with a great work ethic who really want to be a part of the team. Be honest with them and let them know where they stand. Although they will not be able to play on the team, you may be able to offer them other opportunities, such as being the team manager, so that they can still be a part of the team activities.

On the second day of tryouts, split the athletes into two groups: those trying out for junior varsity and those trying out for varsity. After camp and the first day of tryouts, most athletes know which level they would like to try out for. If an athlete is uncertain, make a recommendation based on what you have observed; ultimately, though, the decision is hers. If an athlete gets cut from the varsity tryouts, she should automatically get two more days at the junior varsity level. Generally, though, if a girl is trying out for varsity, her skills are good enough to be selected for the junior varsity team. Some school programs run junior varsity and varsity tryouts together for all sessions. Our program separates them after the first day so that we can focus on smaller groups of athletes.

On the last day of tryouts, meet with your fellow coaches to decide which players to cut and which to keep. Then meet individually with the athletes to inform them of the decisions you have made. Talking individually with the players gives you a chance to address them on a personal level and to genuinely thank them for their effort and hard work.

Role of the Reserve

If ever there was a senior who accepted her role as a reserve, it was Leah. Leah made the varsity team her freshman year as a backup goalkeeper. By her junior year, however, she had given up club soccer and was now playing only a few months of the year. As a result, her skills started to decline. Yet, she always came in fit and really enjoyed being out there with "her girls" and her younger sister, Hannah, who had tremendous talent.

Leah was in good shape, extremely positive, and constantly encouraging the team. We had to take her! She handled the statistics, helped make decisions, and followed through with all the small details of managing a team. She was positive with everyone and had us continually laughing with her stories. By Leah's senior year, we were lucky if she even brought cleats to practice. She was now the third-string goalkeeper, but a first-string teammate. This was a player who stuck around for the two most important reasons: It was fun, and she loved being around her teammates. Leah lettered in soccer as a four-year varsity athlete and earned every bit of that honor.

Player–Coach Meetings

Once you have selected your team, ask the players to fill out a short evaluation form prior to the first day of practice, as shown in figure 17.1. Some players have difficulty determining their goals for the season. The questions on the evaluation form can help get the process started. Remind them that they can reevaluate their goals as the season progresses.

Once you've had an opportunity to read through the evaluations, meet with each player to discuss her form. These meetings can be brief and can take place after practice or after a game. You may have specific questions about something the player wrote on her form, or you can do a general review and let the player guide the discussion based on her needs. Make sure the players' goals are clear and realistic, and let them know that you will review them later in the season or anytime they have concerns.

Although a lot of athletes struggle with the types of questions in figure 17.1, their answers give you a great reference point for evaluating their mental and emotional states in the early stages of the season. Having brief one-on-one meetings with the athletes and discussing their goals, reviewing their off-season commitments, and identifying their strengths shows them you care about their achievements and contributions to the team. These sessions encourage your athletes to express their feelings, ask questions, and trust you with their problems and concerns. Each player's situation is unique; these meetings give you the opportunity to treat each player as a unique individual and help to solidify your relationship.

When players learn how to improve their performance and mental game by committing to their personal goals, they realize that the competition is really about themselves and their own confidence level. Generally, their lack of confidence and commitment are exposed in the evaluations and meetings; this is an important first step in becoming a more complete player. Confidence is based on a player's perceived achievements. You can help your athletes build their confidence by pointing out their small successes and helping them see challenges rather than problems. These evaluations and one-on-one meetings help your athletes gain confidence by focusing on their goals, making realistic commitments, and knowing that they have the support of not only their teammates but their coaching staff as well.

IN-SEASON EVALUATIONS

Preseason evaluations clearly have their place in getting your players off to a good start. You have seen them in camps and tryouts, and you have met with them individually to help them develop goals for the season and examine their levels of commitment and confidence. Now, the season begins. Evaluating your players during the season is obviously a key coaching

Player Preseason Self-Evaluation Form

Name: _____ Date: _____

What is the main strength you can bring to the team?

What do you see as the area that needs the most improvement?

What is your plan to improve in that area?

What specific goals did you set in the off-season?

What goals did you meet, and how will we know whether you've met them?

What are your personal short-term and long-term goals for this season?

What are some team goals you'd like to focus on this season?

Does your confidence make you play well, or does your playing well make you confident?

From *Coaching Girls' Soccer Successfully* by Debra LaPrath, 2009, Champaign, IL: Human Kinetics.

Figure 17.1

responsibility. These evaluations take place in practices, during games, and after games. You can also get some input from the players themselves by giving them a say in the creation of starting lineups.

Practices

Communicating with your players and staff at each practice about goals will help keep everyone alert as to how the players are doing as a team and as individual athletes. You can't be everywhere at once and everything to everyone. To get the most out of your training sessions, use your assistants. Have them help plan and organize the practices. Spending a few minutes before and after practice with your assistants to review and discuss the day's training and any thoughts or concerns about particular athletes can really help you stay on track with your training goals for the week. In addition, student assistants, as well as your injured athletes (unfortunately), can be a great asset in helping you record practice statistics for the evaluation process.

Weekly meetings with your captains can provide feedback on training sessions. Great captains have a finger on the pulse of the team and can let you know exactly how the team is feeling about the training and evaluation sessions. Time spent listening to your captains will not only help to reenergize your team, but also help direct the focus of your planning sessions with your staff. Maybe trainings have been too intense and focused for too long, and the team is feeling burned out. If so, you can make adjustments and add some competitive but fun drills or games that you know the girls enjoy. Maybe your players want more competition within the drills because the focus has been on individual technical skills. At times, it's easy to get so focused on moving forward and achieving your training goals that you forget to step back and let your players have fun and not worry about being evaluated.

Starting Lineup

Another valuable tool in the evaluation process is having athletes suggest the next game's starting lineup. At practice a few days before a game, invite your players to submit suggested lineups. Give each girl a sheet of paper with a diagram of a soccer field and ask her to create a starting lineup with the names of players written on the field in the positions they would play. These written lineups should be anonymous and reviewed only by the coaching staff and the captains. Generally, these lineups reinforce what is already in place; however, you may decide to readjust the lineup based on players' recommendations. Announce the starting lineup on game day after the pregame warm-up.

Games

With no time-outs and no stoppage time (except, of course, in the case of an injury), soccer gives you only a few opportunities to discuss the game with your players. You have a 10-minute halftime after 40 minutes of play, or you can substitute a player out of the game to talk with her during the game. Yelling instructions from the sideline is difficult on players because they are trying to focus on the game while also listening to what you are saying. This can lead to a lot of frustration for both you and the players. If instructions can't wait, keep them as brief and simple as possible. Another option is to send a message with a player who is substituting for another player.

Keeping a statistics book during the game can be helpful for evaluating how the team played as a whole as well as how individual players performed. Record shots on goal including how the goal was scored, assists, fouls, offsides, corner kicks, direct and indirect free kicks, keeper saves, and minutes played by each athlete, as well as field and weather conditions and the names of the referees. For individual athletes, you can track passes completed, passes missed, number of shots, 50-50 balls won and lost, unforced turnovers, give and goes, overlapping runs, take-overs, switched balls, and consecutive passes.

When recording individual statistics, focus on one or two concepts for a more accurate and thorough analysis. For example, we had a forward who was having a difficult time scoring. She felt frustrated and was concerned that she was not getting the ball as much as the other forwards, and therefore not getting the opportunities to finish. We kept a chart of every time she received the ball and where she was on the field during that reception. After reviewing these charts only a few times, she realized that she was in fact getting the opportunity to go to goal. Once she took responsibility for that, she was open-minded and ready to work to find ways to be more successful with those chances.

Keep in contact with the scorekeeper during the game to confirm shots, official times of goals, assists, fouls, and other pertinent information to make sure you are recording these things correctly. At halftime, summarize your statistics so you can accurately discuss what the team has done well so far and what the focus of the second half should be. For example, if a review of the statistics shows that your team has had only one corner kick in the entire 40 minutes of the first half, they need to work harder at forcing more corner kicks, particularly if they are strong in finishing corner kicks.

Although using statistics during your halftime discussion can be helpful, you should simplify the information and focus on only a few important concepts. Bombarding your athletes with too much information will only send them back out on the field frustrated and overwhelmed. Halftime is their only opportunity to regroup as a team and reenergize for the next 40 minutes. Keep your focus for improvement on two or three concepts and compliment them on what they are doing well. (For more information on halftime talks, see chapter 15.)

Another useful tool for evaluating games is video. Although recording soccer games at this level is not as popular as it is in other sports, it can be a great teaching strategy. If you can find a parent who is willing to videotape games (or have the money to hire a professional), you and your staff can use these tapes to evaluate individual and team performance. Such tapes are helpful for addressing mistakes made during the game in a training session. After the coaches have reviewed the video and taken notes, the players can review segments of the video to help them understand key concepts for training. When a player is trying to improve performance, a single image from a video can teach her more than a lengthy explanation.

Postgame

After the game, and after athletes have completed their cool-down, take time to discuss the game briefly. Begin by allowing the athletes to talk about how they think they performed. Ask questions and listen to what the athletes have to say. When asked, "How do you think you played?" athletes have an opportunity to think through and accept responsibility for their performances. Encouraging athletes to talk about what they could have done differently or better opens up a dialogue and allows them to own up to their mistakes and move forward. You may then want to follow up by acknowledging their comments, making recommendations for improved performance, and ending with positive feedback on the things they did well. Consider ending with your hands together and a team cheer to remind each other to let go of today's game and look forward to the next opponent.

CHAPTER 18 EVALUATING YOUR PROGRAM

In addition to evaluating your players, as discussed in chapter 17, evaluating your program at the end of the season is a necessary step in completing your season. Coaches and players observe and evaluate a season from different viewpoints. The evaluation process can be an emotional one for some players, particularly if they believe their contributions to the team were diminished as a result of issues such as a lack of playing time or disciplinary problems. Regardless, evaluations are a necessary process in the growth of coaches, players, and ultimately the program itself.

PLAYER FEEDBACK

During the process of evaluating your program, meet with your players both as a group and individually to revisit preseason team and individual goals. As a head coach, you'll want to evaluate how and when those goals were met, or why they weren't. Having each player complete a program evaluation form (see figure 18.1 on pages 180 and 181) can help you understand their overall experience during the season.

Feedback from veteran players can be invaluable. Be sure to ask them for feedback about their entire careers, not just the current season. Depending on your relationship, you may want to have one-on-one conversations with certain players to give them the opportunity to speak their minds in person. This is a great way to teach young athletes how to communicate with the adults in their lives. Keep in mind, though, that some athletes are not great communicators and would prefer to fill out a written evaluation, particularly if they have criticisms and would have a hard time delivering them face to face.

The information you receive from your veteran players may not always be what you want to hear, but if it can help the program, you'd be wise to listen. Sometimes the heart of a player's criticism is a lack of playing time. In this situation, you must discern her motives and try to put yourself in her shoes, be sensitive to the situation, and try to understand how she is feeling. Veteran players' positive comments, on the other hand, are a welcome sign of support after a long season.

Really listening to your veteran players lets them know that you value their thoughts and opinions. If you've given them the opportunity to express themselves during the season, the evaluation process will not only help the program, but will also give them the closure they need at the end of their careers.

Thank-yous from your players are another important way to evaluate your program. If you aren't hearing *thank you* from time to time, you need to evaluate whether you are using those words yourself. Thank-yous from your players

Girls' Soccer Program Evaluation

Name (optional): _____

Date: _____

The coach communicated her expectations and team rules to players and parents at the beginning of the season.

Strongly agree   Agree   Disagree   Strongly disagree

I felt I had a positive role on the team.

Strongly agree   Agree   Disagree   Strongly disagree

I met my personal goals this season.

Strongly agree   Agree   Disagree   Strongly disagree

The hard work this season was worth it.

Strongly agree   Agree   Disagree   Strongly disagree

The coaches recognized my effort.

Strongly agree   Agree   Disagree   Strongly disagree

Playing this sport helped motivate me to improve my grades.

Strongly agree   Agree   Disagree   Strongly disagree

The coach treated the players with dignity and respect.

Strongly agree   Agree   Disagree   Strongly disagree

The coach was well organized at practices and games.

Strongly agree   Agree   Disagree   Strongly disagree

The coach provided a positive atmosphere during practice sessions and games, which allowed players to improve their abilities.

Strongly agree   Agree   Disagree   Strongly disagree

The coach was knowledgeable about the game of soccer and was able to contribute to the development of the individual players and the team as a whole.

Strongly agree   Agree   Disagree   Strongly disagree

Drills and practices were effective in teaching how to play and perform.

Strongly agree   Agree   Disagree   Strongly disagree

Good sporting behavior was emphasized throughout the season.

Strongly agree   Agree   Disagree   Strongly disagree

Team-building activities interfered with my homework time and therefore my grades suffered.

Strongly agree   Agree   Disagree   Strongly disagree

I am mentally stronger and more confident as a result of playing on this team.

Strongly agree   Agree   Disagree   Strongly disagree

I am physically stronger as a result of playing on this team.

Strongly agree   Agree   Disagree   Strongly disagree

I am technically and tactically better as a result of playing on this team.

Strongly agree   Agree   Disagree   Strongly disagree

I am more conscientious about my lifestyle, such as my nutrition and sleeping habits, as a result of playing on this team.

Strongly agree   Agree   Disagree   Strongly disagree

I understand that everyone has a responsibility to be a leader as a result of playing on this team.

Strongly agree   Agree   Disagree   Strongly disagree

What areas of the program were the most positive and successful that you would not change?

What areas of improvement could be made in the program to provide a better experience for everyone?

Additional comments:

From *Coaching Girls' Soccer Successfully* by Debra LaPrath, 2009, Champaign, IL: Human Kinetics.

Figure 18.1

may come in many forms; they could be verbal or they could be in the form of cards, letters, or invitations. Cards and personal letters of gratitude at the end of the season are a treasured surprise. There is no greater gift than an athlete (or an athlete's parents) taking the time to write a thank-you card or a letter of appreciation. It helps to have those positive letters to reflect on when the opposite happens and the criticism comes in, and it will.

What matters most is that you learn from your mistakes and don't repeat them. Getting both positive feedback and criticism helps you grow as a coach. Getting invitations in the mail from former players who are graduating from college, getting married, or having baby showers is another reminder of the positive relationships that were formed during their time in your program. These invitations are probably the

greatest reward of all because even as the years have passed, these young women still consider you an important part of their lives!

STAFF FEEDBACK

Regardless of the type of season you've had, it is important to evaluate your program both on your own and with your assistant coaches. You owe it to yourself and your assistant coaches to sit down with them and get their feedback at the end of the season.

When evaluating your program, you and your assistant coaches should fill out a staff evaluation form, as shown in figure 18.2. By sitting down and honestly answering these and similar questions, you will discover which changes you need to make and which aspects of your

Girls' Soccer Coaching Staff Evaluation

Name: _____ Position: _____

Date: _____

Do all members of the coaching staff have the same values as you do? If not, what differences did you experience?

How did the team do with the talent it had? Did it exceed or fall short of its vision and expectations?

Were the team goals appropriate given the level of talent and experience?

Did you lead by example (e.g., in attitude, enthusiasm, work ethic, and lifestyle)?

Did you encourage and develop leadership skills in your athletes?

What direction is your program heading?

Were there any situations that you could have handled better or in a different way?

From *Coaching Girls' Soccer Successfully* by Debra LaPrath, 2009, Champaign, IL: Human Kinetics.

Figure 18.2

program can be left alone. Keep in mind that this process is to help you grow as a coach and a person; it is not a guarantee that your next season will be without fault. The next season will be an entirely different journey, with a different group and a new set of ups and downs.

If you are close with your staff, an evaluation does not have to be a formal procedure. Meeting in person over dinner or coffee can be a great way to evaluate the program. You may even find yourselves talking for hours and becoming energized and excited to start the next season (which is seven months away)! If you do not have a close relationship with your assistants, a written evaluation may be the best way to get their honest opinions.

Whether you evaluate your staff through a written evaluation or a verbal face-to-face meeting, make sure you are thorough and honest. It doesn't help them or the program to sugarcoat their performances if you were not satisfied. Tell them what you observed as their strengths and how those strengths benefited the team. Then review what you observed as their weaknesses while recommending ways for them to improve in those areas. If they have fallen short of your expectations in several areas, or were more of a hindrance than a help, it may be time for them to pursue another program. Offer that suggestion only once you've given them the opportunity to work through their shortcomings.

INDEX

Note: An *f* following a page number refers to a figure.

ABOUT THE AUTHOR

Debra LaPrath has been head coach at California's Maria Carrillo High School since 1996. She has led MCHS to six consecutive North Coast Section finals and won back-to-back championships in 2001 and 2002. LaPrath earned North Coast Section Coach of the Year honors in 2004, along with various conference and media Coach of the Year honors in 1998, 1999, 2000, 2001, and 2002. She is a member of the National Soccer Coaches Association of America; the California Association of Health, Physical Education, Recreation and Dance; and the National Education Association. LaPrath grew up in San Diego playing for the San Diego Surf Soccer Club and moved to Sonoma County to play Soccer for Sonoma State University. She has coached for more than 18 years. In addition to her on-field success, LaPrath uses a variety of fund-raising, team-building, and community service projects to give her athletes a well-rounded experience and create a program that is greater than any one achievement. LaPrath believes it's most important to focus on helping to raise confident, happy young women. She lives in Rohnert Park, California.

You'll find other outstanding soccer resources at

http://soccer.humankinetics.com

In the U.S. call 1-800-747-4457

Australia 08 8372 0999 • Canada 1-800-465-7301
Europe +44 (0) 113 255 5665 • New Zealand 0064 9 448 1207

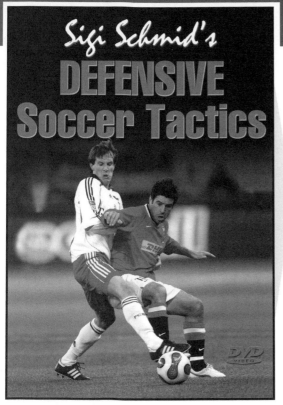